THE FEDERAL ELECTION COMMISSION

Policy, Politics, and Administration

Maurice C. Sheppard

University Press of America,® Inc.
Lanham · Boulder · New York · Toronto · Plymouth, UK

Copyright © 2007 by
University Press of America,® Inc.
4501 Forbes Boulevard
Suite 200
Lanham, Maryland 20706
UPA Acquisitions Department (301) 459-3366

Estover Road
Plymouth PL6 7PY
United Kingdom

Library of Congress Control Number: 2006922531
ISBN-13: 978-0-7618-3456-4 (paperback : alk. paper)
ISBN-10: 0-7618-3456-7 (paperback : alk. paper)

Contents

List of Tables and Figures

Acknowledgments

I sincerely thank the following individuals for their professional and personal assistance regarding this book. To my Alma College and Ripon College colleagues, thank you for editorial comments. To my mother and father, Kathleen and John Sheppard, and the entire Sheppard family, thank you for believing in me. To Holly and Isaiah Davis, thank you for your moral and spiritual support that allowed me to complete this work.

Introduction

Because public policy is not self-executing, administrative agencies are necessary to facilitate the proper processing, implementation, and enforcement of democratically constructed law. This book looks at the administrative processing of federal campaign finance regulation by analyzing the administrative behavior of the Federal Election Commission (FEC). This research is important because it contributes toward developing a better understanding of the distinctive relationship between policy issues and their implementation by an administrative agency in the context of democratic government and politics. The analysis contends that administrative arrangements (i.e., structure and management arrangements) as determined by political officials relating to the particular public policy produce predictable outcomes that may be inconsistent with the goals of a democratic society. Results presented in this book not only complement the existing literature by clarifying complex political-administrative relationships, but also highlight why administrative agency administration of public policy matter regarding democratic outcomes. Specifically, this book analyzes if regulation and enforcement of the federal campaign finance system by the FEC produces policy outcomes consistent with democratic theory and government in the United States. Discussion of issues concerning administration and enforcement of campaign finance regulation are part of addressing the general political-administrative research question motivating this book: What is the relationship between a public policy and its administration in the context of democratic government and politics?

Before discussing the significance, objectives, and plan of the book, it is necessary to put the discussion of campaign finance regulation in its proper place. The issue of campaign finance regulation as discussed in this book focuses on the topic of organizational administration of legitimate public policy as designated by elected officials. The analysis presented in this book does not advocate a particular type of campaign finance reform that benefits liberal or conservative, democrat or republican. Analysis, comments, and discussions contained in this book advocate the protection and expansion of fundamental democratic rights of all citizens in the United States to fully participate in free and open elections. At best, this book stresses that campaign finance regulatory administration should enhance democratic freedoms and processes. This book focuses on campaign finance regulation administration by the FEC and if its actions impede or enhance democratic rights and freedoms.

Significance of the Research

Money in politics is an important public issue as the specter of formal and informal *quid-pro-quo* systems remain a topic of contemporary campaign and election debate (Sabato and Simpson 1996). Along with increasing criticism of government efforts to regulate campaign financing in the United States, the FEC has increasingly become the target of public ridicule. Of particular interest regarding the regulation of the campaign finance system are questions about the relationship between political officials and government regulators. Specifically, if this political-administrative relationship might hamper FEC staff and leadership from vigorously investigating reported violations of campaign finance law (Oldaker 1986; Hamilton 1994). While politicians debate the content of campaign finance regulation, administration and enforcement of these laws occurs only when the FEC takes action.

As an administrative agency, the FEC—as established by the 1974 Amendments to the Federal Election Campaign Act (FECA)—has the unique duty of administrating and enforcing campaign finance laws that political officials in the legislative, executive, and judicial branches of government may dispute. Thus, there is a contradiction when one considers that FEC administration and enforcement of campaign finance law might run counter to the desires of political officials within the government institutions that created and sustain the agency (Johnson 1992). Accordingly, this book addresses the following question: Does the structural and management arrangements of the FEC, as determined by political officials, produce policy outcomes that are inconsistent with normative assumptions of democratic theory and government?

Along with addressing this theoretical question, the book also deals with a more concrete issue: Is there evidence to show how organizational decision-makers at the FEC administratively respond to multiple political constraints? Political-administrative relationships are an integral part of a larger contextual environment that shapes organizational decision-making processes. Thus, in order to understand the ad-

ministrative behavior of an agency like the FEC over time, it is necessary to examine its relationship to political officials in the context of
democratic government and politics.

The basic assumption underlying this research is that the FEC operates in a politically motivated environment that potentially prevents
the organization from implementing and producing policy outcomes
that are consistent with democratic goals. If the data and analysis presented in this book support this assumption, we should find that while
the FEC provides meaningful symbolic regulatory administration and
enforcement functions, because of its unique structural and management arrangements, the agency fails to produce policy outcomes consistent with the lofty goals originally envisioned for it when established
in 1974. If this is the case, we might conclude that regardless of future
reforms (i.e., contribution limits, coordinated expenditures, issue advocacy), until the structural and management arrangements of the FEC
change in a manner that allows agency personnel to provide effective
and efficient administration and enforcement, the issue of money in
politics will remain contentious. Efforts to maintain the legitimacy of
the campaign finance system, therefore, will remain hollow so long as
the FEC remains feckless.

Objectives

This book has four primary objectives. First, provide a careful and
thoughtful overview of the relationship between different types of democratic theories, views of citizenship, and corresponding models of
policy-making in the United States. This overview is important regarding the question of whether public policies are developed and implemented for the benefit of the many or for the few. By outlining competing theories of democracy and the commonly held views concerning
the role of citizens in the democratic process, this book provides a
pragmatic analysis and explanation of how government processes
might lead to the implementation of specific types of policies and by
extension administrative arrangements. In addition, analyzing public
knowledge of government and politics provide empirical data that allows for a meaningful discussion about the diverse nature of public
policies and why some specific public interest groups might use their
information advantage toward shaping the public policy process. Ultimately, however, what the analysis highlights is that particular public
policies are more consistent with a particular theory of democracy and
view of citizenship that lead to predictable government agency administrative arrangements and policy outcomes.

Second, present a careful analysis of the FEC as the regulatory agency that implements and enforces federal regulation within an intense political environment. Studying the administrative arrangements of the FEC provides an opportunity to analyze just how the policy process relating to a federal regulatory agency operating at the heart of the political process (Jackson 1990; Ripley 1967, 1986; Ripley and Franklin 1991). The duties and responsibilities of the FEC include enforcing federal campaign finance laws that might be contradictory to the desires of political officeholders and their related interested in the legislative, executive, and judicial branches of the federal government (Oldaker 1986). Although the FEC undertake duties similar to traditional regulatory agencies, such as the Federal Communications Commission (FCC) or the Federal Trade Commission (FTC) in regulating an industry, the FEC is nonetheless different in that it regulates a unique policy area—politics. Analyzing the unique features of the FEC in this context allows for the possibility of developing a more general statement about the democratic nature of administrative implementation of public policy. This overview of the FEC, in addition, provides important historical insight into the complex nature of administrating and enforcing campaign finance law in the United States. Note that among the world's large industrialized democracies, only the United States has a federal-level regulatory body dedicated to the administration and enforce campaign finance law in federal elections (Gunlicks 1993).

Third, analyze the structure and management arrangements of the FEC to develop a better understanding of the complex role administrative agencies, such as the FEC, play in the policy process and related policy outcomes. Due to the diverse nature of public policies and administrative agencies, it is necessary to consider that despite detailed policy language, particular administrative arrangements may lead to policy outcomes that are inconsistent with democratic theory and government. Earlier research analyzing political-administrative relationships sometime have not always fully accounted for the diverse nature of policy issues and the corresponding structural and management arrangements. While large and complex regulatory agencies such as the Environmental Protection Agency (EPA), Food and Drug Administration (FDA), and Securities and Exchange Commission (SEC) have undergone extensive analysis, two general questions remain. First, do regulatory agencies with relatively simple hierarchical structures respond in the same manner to political influence as large, complex regulatory agencies? Second, do management arrangements concerning agency enforcement style and resources matter regarding the degree to which political officials might influence enforcement activities? Data about administrative arrangements–structural and managerial–are important in the case of the FEC since this is the agency responsible for maintaining the legitimacy of the federal campaign finance system. The administrative arrangements of the FEC may determine political winners and losers that set government policy agendas and alternatives (Kingdon 1984).

Fourth, provide a general discussion regarding the importance of administrative arrangements to policy implementation that produces outcomes consistent with the tenets of democratic theory and government. This book discusses democracy in the United States without entangling itself in partisan and ideological debates. Therefore, by questioning and analyzing exclusively fundamental issues of democracy, policy, interests, and administration, this book addresses the unfinished business of safeguarding individual rights and equality that are central to theories of democracy. If the research infers that policy issues relating to campaign finance regulation produce administrative arrangements that threaten democratic rights, then public officials, policy experts, and concerned citizens may use this information to help develop new arrangements that reverse this trend. This information underscores that point that different public policies require distinctive administrative arrangements to ensure that policy implementation by public organizations produce policy outcomes consistent with the goals of a democratic society.

To achieve this end, data in this book represent FEC administrative behavior and elements of the agency's administrative arrangements. All data are public and collected under the Freedom of Information Act from the FEC and other public sources. Analysis of selected data uses elements of quantitative and qualitative methodologies to provide as unbiased findings as possible. This mixed approach facilitates a more open and critical analysis of the data.

Finally, because of a conscious effort by the author to minimize misinterpreting the facts or analysis while enhancing the readability of the book, normally complex concepts, ideas, and relationships are at times presented as simply and clearly as possible. Thus, it is hoped that the benefits of simplifying complex issues, ideas, and concepts does not come at the cost of reducing the book's overall intellectual and academic value. In the end, however, this or any book is only as valuable as its ability to disseminate ideas that challenge individuals and society to think critically about the choices we make.

Plan of the Book

The book provides the following analysis. Chapter 1 presents a general overview and discussion of the democratic theory and models of policy-making. Chapter 2 discusses the level of knowledge citizens have about government and why this matters concerning political processing of public policy and the administrative arrangements of the FEC. Chapter 3 is a historical overview of efforts in the United States to regulate money in federal elections. This information is important toward developing an accurate contextual picture of government efforts over time to regulate money in politics and the creation of the FEC. Chapter 4 provides a theoretical overview of the FEC and its relationship to political officials by demonstrating the value of organization theory in the analysis of public organizations. Chapter 5 presents a detailed account of the structural and managerial arrangements of the FEC regarding the administration and enforcement of campaign finance law. This particular overview, while similar in some respects to past research regarding administrative arrangements, is nonetheless unique in that it provides a specific and meaningful analysis of how the administrative arrangements of the FEC relate to the agency's measurable policy outputs. Chapter 6 briefly outlines the development of the literature on political-administrative relationships and offers testable hypotheses evolving from the relevant literature and FEC information. Chapter 7 is an analysis of empirical organization-level data about the relationship between FEC enforcement activity and elected official manipulation of agency resources. Presentation of case studies and longitudinal statistical data attempt to put structural and managerial arrangements in their appropriate political and historical context concerning FEC administrative behavior. The expectation is that the analysis in this chapter presents evidence that support the underlining assumption of this book. This assumption is as follows: That due to the fundamental nature of some public policy issues (i.e., campaign financing) and tense political-administrative relationships (i.e., FEC and political officials), particular administrative arrangements (i.e., FEC structure and management arrangements) are instituted that lead to policy outcomes that might be inconsistent with democratic goals (i.e., competitive elections). Finally, chapter 8 summarizes the analysis and provides guidance regarding contributions of this analysis to the study of political-administrative relationship.

Chapter I

Democratic Theory and Models of Policy-Making

Campaign finance regulation attempts to achieve effective freedom of speech that does not provide a disproportional advantage to any particular political group or interest. Nonetheless, concerns about application of the law, definition of expenditure, and restrictions on contributions abound (Arneson 1982). FEC administration and enforcement of campaign finance law involves difficult theoretical and practical issues concerning their implementation. That said, what if evidence concludes that administration and enforcement of campaign finance law by the FEC produces or allows policy outcomes inconsistent with conventional notions of democratic theory and government? If such evidence does exist it would prove valuable toward correcting these "undemocratic" outcomes and toward the development of more accurate political-administrative models.

This chapter looks at fundamental theoretical models concerning democratic theory and the democratic nature of public policy processing and implementation. First, there is an overview of the meaning and scope of democratic theory in the context of the United States. Second, there is an examination of policy-making models and criteria for evaluation to clearly identify why the policy process is important regarding possible undemocratic policy outcomes. Third, the chapter concludes with a discussion regarding the implications of policy implementation according to a particular model of policy-making in reference to campaign finance law and the FEC.

Fragmented Nature of Democratic Theory

Democratic theory and government require popular sovereignty, equality among citizens, consultation between government and citizens over proposed major courses of action, and majority rule. Democratic theory and government, in addition, requires elements such as freedom of expression, citizen participation in decision-making, uncensored mass media to hold government accountable for its decisions, an independent judiciary, and regular free elections encouraging participation and political accountability. While the degrees to which these elements found in a democracy vary according to social, historical, and cultural contexts, these are nonetheless necessary if not sufficient to maintain formal institutions.

American democratic theory follows the political philosophy and classic liberal ideas of John Locke (1632-1704). Locke focuses on issues such as role of rationality, consent, individualism, rule of law, natural law, religion, majority rule, right of revolution, and property rights. According to Locke, the securing of natural rights is government's primary purpose, noting that if a government exceeds its legitimate limits citizens have the right to break the "social contract" and revolt. These ideas, along with references to self-evident truths, the equality of men, and inalienable rights such as life and liberty inform the basis for Thomas Jefferson's drafting the *Declaration of Independence* (1776) and James Madison's extensive development of the *U.S. Constitution* (1787). However, understanding the depth and complexity of Locke's theory of democratic government in the context of the United States requires disassembling the theory. This is necessary to understand and appreciate variations of democratic theory that matter regarding the making and implementation of public policy in the United States (Holden 1988). Locke's liberal democracy in the United States offers two views concerning the role citizens should play in a democracy—the active view and the consent view (Table 1.1).

Table 1.1.   Types of Liberal Democratic Theory

Citizenship	Moral	Types of Democracy Protective	Development
Consent View	Institutional	Madisonian	Private
Active View	Communicative	Jeffersonian	Participatory

Source: Hoffman, T. (1998). "Rationality Reconceived." *Critical Review, 12,* 459-480.

The consent view of citizenship develops from Locke's notion of the ultimate consent of the people. This concept of the role of the citizen in democratic government is in accordance with the idea of a kind of political *division of labor*. This division of labor would be between government officials and all citizens in that there is less of a demand on citizens concerning their role and direct participation in governmental affairs. Under this view, citizens are not required to use a great deal of their intellectual abilities to evaluate the actions of public officials who function as caretakers.

The active view of citizenship, in contrast, carries with it a critical concept of the role of citizens in government. According to this view, deficiencies in individual-level political sophistication are serious challenges to democratic legitimacy and relates to Locke's right of popular revolt as justification for citizens in relationship to government. It is this notion of citizens' right to revolt against government that provides support for the idea of routine citizen engagement in governmental and political affairs as advocated by contemporary political philosophy (Holden 1988).

Both the consent and active view of citizenship extend across three distinctive types of democratic theory. *Moral theories* of democracy claim some part of government is inherently necessary for expressing basic moral goodness as determined by some natural law. Types under this theory include Kant's-consent view (institutional) and Habermas (1990) active view (communicative) (Christiano 1996). *Protective theories* of democracy claim some aspect of government is inherently necessary for the protection of some other good that is not inherently required for the operation of democracy itself. Types under this theory include Madison's consent view (complex institutions) and Jefferson's-active view (simple institutions). *Developmental theories* of democracy claim some aspect of government is inherently necessary for the proper development of the individual to become a self-determining being. Types under this theory include Downs' (1957) consent view (private) and Sandel's (1996) active view (participatory). While no single view of citizenship according to the various theories of democracy is absolute, drawing distinctions among and across these ideas provides a helpful outline for understanding why conversations about citizenship and government responsibility rarely result in meaningful or productive deliberation (Hoffman 1998).

Citizens, nonetheless, can delegate political roles to representatives and remain consistent with an active view of citizenship as a means to achieve policy goals. However, citizens must, at a minimum, be able and willing to engage in deliberations about which social issue government should address and their corresponding public policy that clearly outlines, analyzes, processes, and evaluates. Consistent with ideas of self-determination, individuals cannot delegate this fundamental responsibility onto others without renouncing the very feature that justifies their rights in the first place (Christiano 1996). Accordingly, supposed collective political rationality is insufficient because political preferences concerning policy goals may originate in the cumulative influence of special interest-driven political discourse. Because special interest influence may be responsible for the content of public discourse and policy preferences about policy goals, it is unreasonable to expect aggregate preferences to meet the demands of democratic theory (Zaller 1992). Thus, it seems reasonable to conclude there might be a special interest bias regarding public policy agendas, development, and implementation (Bachrach 1980; Finocchiaro 1999). At this point, it is necessary to examine what this special interest bias might mean to policy-making and administration.

Models of Policy-Making

Before reviewing and discussing models of policy-making in the context of the United States, it is important to note what public policy is and is not. At its most fundamental level, public policy is what government does or does not do regarding an identifiable social issue. Decisions and procedures concerning the collection and use of public resources to implement a government solution do not take place in a void. Public policy is the outcome of purposeful government efforts to implement legitimate electorate demands to correct or address some societal problem through formal institutional procedures. This process takes the following electoral form: (a) candidates can offer competing policy alternatives; (b) voters cast ballots based on policy preferences; (c) election outcomes reflect a policy preference; and (d) winning candidates attempt to enact the electorate policy preference. Thus, despite popular anti-government claims about the legitimacy of government action, there is evidence that government does respond to public concerns. (Note: While questions about the legitimacy of these procedures and processes might be valid, their analysis is beyond the scope of this research.) Democratic government, in theory, attempts to act in a purposeful, goal-oriented manner that produces policy inputs that correct societal problems targeted for government action by elected officials while producing outcomes consistent with democratic theory and government.

Typically, studies of public policy-making include a series of orderly stages that occur within government and the political system.

This process usually occurs in the following identifiable stages. First, there is the identification stage at which time consideration of a policy problem by government begins. Second, the agenda-setting stage involving policy-makers and staff prioritizing issues to address. Third, there is the policy formulation stage where proposals begin to take shape and develop by policy-planning organizations, interest groups, government administrations, and elected officials. Fourth, there is the legitimization stage at which time policies go through political actions (i.e., public hearings) at which stakeholders officially state their support or objection for a proposed policy. Fifth, the implementation stage requires a public organization (i.e., agency, commission, or department) to use public resources for policy implementation to correct the identified problem. Sixth, the evaluation stage calls for a review of policy impact on the target population and identify any unintended consequences (Kingdon 1984). Questions about how the policy process itself begins and proceeds require a review of two prominent policy-making models: the bottom-up model and the top-down model (Dye 2002).

Bottom-Up Model

Referred to as the bottom-up model, this *pluralist view* assumes that in a modern democracy mass or popular identification of social problems and issues are introduced into the political and policy process for discussion, consideration, debate, and resolution. Accordingly, individuals can and do define their own interests, organize themselves, persuade others to support their cause, gain access to government officials, influence institutional decision-making, and watch over administrative implementation of government policies. The exercise of popular approval or disapproval for the outcome of any particular public policy is evident through the electoral system.

This model assumes that interest groups function as intermediaries between individuals and government. Interest groups supplement the election system by providing individuals with the means of directly influencing government policy-making. Political parties then organize popular majorities and grassroots efforts to exercise influence over government policy action. In order for mass influence on government policy-makers to be effective, parties need to be *responsible* in the sense that they are responsive to popular policy sentiments. For parties to be responsible they must (a) recruit candidates (b) present workable policies, (c) organize campaigns, and (d) implement policies proposed during campaigns.

This model contends that the most important policy-making activities occur within government. Specifically, government institutions such as Congress, the president, and the Supreme Court, and bureaucracy respond to multiple political, institutional, and interest group pressure during the policy-making process. It is during this process that these contextual factors produce collective pressure on elected and politically appointed officeholders in a manner that influence policy identification, agenda setting, formulation, legitimacy, implementation, and evaluation. This traditional model, based on conventional wisdom grounded in popular democratic theory, views the policy-making process as a series of activities initiated from below.

The environmental movement in the United States serves as an example of this bottom-up model in action. Beginning with the publication of Rachel Knight's *Silent Spring* (1962), sufficient grassroots effort began to expose large-scale environmental pollution by using collective action measures (e.g., campaigns, protests, public hearings). Due to this mass effort and growing support of political officials, President Richard Nixon and a Democratic Congress established the EPA in 1972 to take administrative responsibility for regulation and enforcing old and new environmental standards. An important feature of this policy area is that in many cases because the problems are regional and national in nature possible solutions to identifiable problems call for complex intergovernmental and private industry action.

Top-Down Model

The top-down policy-making model describes a process in which special interest groups transmit their values and preferences into the policy process via the broader society. The most practical manner to conceive of this *elite view* of special interest-driven policy-making is to view the process as a separate path by which the policy preferences of the socioeconomic elite filter to and through the broader society below. While there is some disconnection in these processes, communication of elite-driven policy preferences occurs through each stage of the policy process. Specialized interest groups representing various political, social, and economic elite interests begin by identifying policies that are most important to them.

In this top-down model, elite special interests pressure elected and appointed public policy-makers to support narrowly tailored policies that favor elite interest and preferences. These interest groups are organizations that seek to influence government policy to obtain special benefits, subsidies, privileges, and protections for their sponsors. According to Thomas Dye (2002) they may be responsible to the same corporate, banking, financial, professional, legal, media, and multiple civic institutions that compose something akin to a national special interest. In addition, this top-down process includes the distribution of campaign funds to elected officials and political candidates. While these contributions may not buy votes, at the very least, they may pay for access and influence.

This model, in general, assumes that identifying what issues are societal problems and setting an agenda for analysis and discussion of these issues is more important than deciding the solution. Conditions in society not identifiable by special interests as problems, according to this model, therefore rarely receive adequate media attention to gain the support of the public or political officials to get on the government's policy agenda. It is important to understand that this top-down perspective of the policy-making process does not render bottom-up popular policy sentiment meaningless. What it does accomplish, however, is to frame the debate about which issues are placed on governments decision-making agenda and the prioritization of these problems for setting policy analysis, deliberate, alternatives, and subsequent resource allocation.

One issue that illustrates elite-driven policy agenda and alternatives is tax policy. At the very foundation of government activity, the issue of revenue collection has and continues be to of intense interest to all segments of the population. In the United States, while there have been periods of heightened consideration regarding extensive reform of the federal tax code, for the most part, these reform efforts have focused on general levels of taxation and their progressive or regressive nature. Regardless, much more complex, and some would argue, more important tax policy loopholes remain either untouched or receive only marginal attention. These tax policy loopholes have been and continue to be the privy of the elite segment in society.

The issue of bottom-up or top-down policy-making process matters because policy identification and interest involvement in the public policy process determines social and economic "winners" and "losers." While government organizations are limited in their ability to make policy, they do have the effective equivalent during the policy implementation stage of the policy process. Elected officials, politically appointed administrators, and organized stakeholders monitoring of administrative agencies insure these public organizations do not drift too far from their institutionally determined roles and activities.

Of particular interest is the significance of a top-down model as elite special interest groups may attempt to influence policy-makers to narrow the scope of their activities in a manner that is overtly advantageous to them and covertly disadvantageous to the non-elite regarding election policy. What are the political consequences of a policy process that follows a top-down model for producing policy outcomes consistent with democratic theory and government?

Policy Implications of a Top-Down Process

There are two important implications about top-down policy-making. First, top-down policy-making is compatible with democratic theory. Constitutional safeguards limit special interests from infringing on basic liberties that are the rightful claim of all democratic citizens. The basis for this claim is that constitutional arrangements support the principle of government by the consent of the people through open, free, periodic, and competitive elections that allow popular majorities to replace government leaders. The top-down policy-making model is most compatible with the consent view of citizenship as listed in Table 1.1. Under this division of labor view, citizens in free and open elections select political leaders according to a candidate's policy agenda, ideological position, and political skill to promote and establish public policies that may be consistent with their own views. The types of democracies listed in Table 1.1 that the top-down process is most consistent with would depend upon the policy type and context. A public policy such as campaign finance regulation would possibly fall under the heading of a protective theory of democracy. This type would emphasize defending the integrity of the campaign finance system for purpose of preventing the potential destructive nature of money in politics. While a top-down model appears consistent with a consent view of citizenship, the issue remains open regarding how much freedom policy-makers should have regarding policy matters that are of public and private interests simultaneously.

Second, top-down policy-making does not replace bottom-up policy-making, but only provides another abstract approach for viewing the multi-dimensional policy-making process in a more realistic manner. This is important because due to the diversity of policies, the processing and implementation of specific policies vary. It does not seem reasonable to assume that all public policy take the same path from conceptual birth to administrative implementation. A top-down policy-making model simply provides another way to analyze complex policy-making in a democracy from a different perspective that realistically accounts for policy types, stakeholders, political officials, and general social context than linear perspectives. A top-down model, nonetheless, does imply that policy might not reflect the demands of the broader society so much as the interests of a select elite.

Such has been the charge from those advocating extensive campaign finance reform. In general, both liberal and conservative proponents contend that current campaign finance law is bias in favor of incumbent political officials maintaining their public office in order to serve a narrow range of social, economic, and faith-based interests. These competing positions regarding campaign finance reform seem to differ primarily on the issues correlating to a cost-benefit analysis. In essence, both proponents seek reform that (a) benefits their own interest while simultaneously (b) establishing institutional and administrative measures that raise costs for their opponent.

Ramifications for Policy Implementation and Oversight

What does a top-down model mean then regarding how government organizations implement public policy? In essence, it seems that a top-down policy process, depending upon the particular policy and political context, could put an administration agency somewhere along a policy implementation continuum. At one end, the agency benefits from widespread political and popular support that enhances visibility of its actions and insulates the organization from intense, narrow scrutiny. This would seem to be consistent with a bottom-up policy process. At the other end of the continuum, agencies with little affirmative political and popular support for its actions are vulnerable to attack from hostile political and special interest groups. This would seem to be consistent with a top-down policy process. Regarding campaign and election policy, an administrative agency such as the FEC might find itself institutionally biased toward the latter end of the continuum rather than the former, particularly concerning policy oversight.

Policy oversight by political officials establishes procedural requirements in a decentralized institutional setting for monitoring administrative behavior. McCubbins and Schwartz (1984) make this distinction by using two ideal forms of oversight. First, *police-patrol* oversight is analogous to the use of real police patrols that is centralized, active, and direct. Thus, like police officials, political officials examine a sample of agency activities, with the intent of detecting and correcting actions that might pose a barrier toward achieving their political and policy goals. It is through this ongoing surveillance activity that political officials can discourage such actions. The survey of agency activity may take various forms (e.g., documents, commissions, field observations, and hearings) by political officials to prevent administrative disturbance.

Second, there is *fire-alarm* oversight that is analogous to the use of real fire alarms. This oversight approach is less centralized and reduces political intervene in the administrative process when compared to the police-patrol approach. Instead of continually examining a sample of administrative actions, looking for violations of political goals, institutional officials establish a system of rules, procedures, and practices that enable individual and organized groups to periodically examine administrative action themselves. This model allows outside interests to charge agencies with violating political goals, and seek remedies from political institutions and organizations. Political officials oversee this decentralized system and intervene only when responding to formal complaints.

This distinction between police-patrol and fire alarm oversight, nonetheless, might not provide a clear or realistic explanation of how political officials with oversight responsibilities might use one or both of these abstract oversight approaches. For example, what is the link (if any) between the oversight approach political officials use, the policy itself, and the broader socioeconomic context? In addition, do political officials switch between oversight-types over time depending on the nature of the policy issue, socioeconomic context, and political actors? For instance, is it reasonable to expect incumbent members of Congress to be proactive or reactive regarding specific policy issues that directly affect their re-election prospects? This matter is not only important to the particular officeholder, but also to the elected officials' constituents, party colleagues, and policy supporters. The point is that while the usefulness of oversight types is limited they nonetheless are helpful tools that allow us to better understand how political officials respond to a particular policy issue such as campaign finance regulation.

Regarding federal election regulation, any reform of the *status quo* campaign finance system in theory constitutes a threat to incumbent officeholders and related interests. Reform of the campaign finance system would increase incumbent officials' uncertainty regarding future campaign and election success. It is only reasonable to expect incumbent policy-makers to remain intensely aware of any proposed reform or change of campaign finance law no matter how minor a possible reform may appear. Thus, while these oversight-types are useful tools for understanding political determination of administrative oversight procedures and processes, their usefulness is of limited value if not viewed in a meaningful context. The use of oversight-types is only useful if analyzed in reference to a specific political policy issue such as campaign financing, and policy-making model.

Evaluation of a Policy-Model Relationship

It would be misleading to claim that all public policies follow either exclusively a bottom-up or a top-down model in terms of their processing on two points. First, there is the practical reality that policy issues and their related processing are extremely complex and rarely allow themselves to simple, one-dimensional analysis and remedy. It seems farcical to insist, for example, that economic policy could be effectively developed and implemented absent review and adjustment of employment policy in the broader social and political context. Second, there is the acknowledgment that claiming there is only one or the other policy model is to commit an "either" "or" fallacy. This simply means that beyond the strict guidelines of formal theoretical modeling, it is quite improbable that individuals encounter situations in which there is only one 'right answer.' Therefore, due to the complex realities and uncertainties a 'single-best' policy-model regarding a specific policy issue is not recommended. A more systematic approach, therefore, is necessary.

Assuming the above statement is correct, then a possible course of action to untangle this issue might be to (a) identify a specific policy issue; (b) recognize formal institutional-organizational participants; and (c) highlight specific influential interests and stakeholders. This systematic approach offers the possibility of producing a clearer picture of what might be the most appropriate policy-model and oversight approach to use regarding analyzing political oversight of administrative agency actions and relevant political-administrative relationships that provide information about policy implementation and how consistent policy outcomes are with democratic theory. That said, debate regarding the use of these ideal-types continues due to issue complexity. These models, nonetheless, do help us clarify an otherwise incomprehensible process.

To develop this point, compare the different political and issue settings between environmental policy and education policy. It seems practical to assume that interests active in either of these two policy areas would be measurably different. On the one hand, those involved in environmental policy are concerned with matters and resources that are broad and diverse in scope. Due to the diverse nature of environmental issues, depending upon a specific issue area, each level of government in the United States—local, state, regional, and federal—are all involved to different degrees depending upon the type of problem and interest involvement. On the other hand, those involved in education policy focus their attention and resources much more narrowly at the local level of government. Due to existing legislative structures, the hub of education policy development and implementation is predominantly at the local level with some state and federal involvement, particularly concerning issues such as schools of choice. While some overlap does occur, these areas are separate and distinct (Gerber and Teske 2000). What this means is that the evaluation of a policy-model relationship and oversight approach regarding a particular policy issue requires careful attention to a broad range of issue related matters.

Even so, there seems to be three additional points that are relevant to even a cursory evaluation of a possible policy-model relationship and oversight approach. First, there is *policy complexity*: Is the policy issue and significance readily understood by average informed, rational persons? Some policies, by their very nature may tend to be more complex and therefore require greater technical expertise than other policy areas to adequately understand the issue (e.g., campaign contributions and "in-kind" contributions). In some cases, it is simply not practical to expect the average individual or voter to understand adequately the substance of the policy issues in order to make a thoughtful and reasoned decision.

Second, there is *policy scope*: How expansive is the policy problem as it affects the broader community? For instance, attempts to address environmental policy concerning global warming, in some cases, have an almost fundamental link to other policy areas such as the economy, education, and health. While no policy exists in isolation of other policy areas, some issues, due in part to the nature of the matter, tend to have a broader scope than others. For instance, while campaign finance policy affects a narrow interest (e.g., political candidates) there is also the claim that it influences the broader policy-making process itself (e.g., elected officials). While some will contend that every policy area involves a broad review of its content, it might be the policy process itself that determines the scope of the policy.

Third, there is *policy interest*: Who is interested in the policy issue? Different policies have unique constituencies that may (or may not) have special political, financial, social, and personal interests concerning the development and implementation of the specific public policy. This closely relates to the notion of political intensity (i.e., some groups in society are more prone to policy action due to their attachment to a particular policy issue). Debate regarding campaign finance regulation, for instance, usually pits ideologically driven and well-financed political interests against one another in zero-sum contests for public office. In some cases, this might mean a coalition of traditional adversaries develops in an attempt to maintain their *status quo* positions in the political firmament. Other times, this might mean that historical alliances suddenly find themselves pitted against one another due to significant ideological differences.

In the end, policy complexity, scope, and interest might provide reasonable criteria for evaluating the reasonableness of a policy-model relationship. How might using these criteria be useful in the analysis of the FEC and evaluating the democratic nature of its policy output?

Implications for the FEC

The FEC, due to the complexity of campaign finance regulation, scope of influence, and interests concerning election policy, probably resides more often than not at the police-patrol end of the oversight continuum for several reasons. First, due to issues of complexity, popular discussion of campaign finance policy is confused. Thus, the administrative agency is in a real sense left alone to face these political interests who are very mindful of this issue, absent well-defined popular support for administrative officials. Second, while the true scope of election policy (campaign finance regulation specifically) is extensive, popular discussion and debate of the topic is narrow. Election policy is not just about who wins office, but more importantly, what elected officials do once in office. Rarely is the discussion of election policy put into the broader and much more important context that elected officials possess a truly extensive range of coercive public power. Third, absent popular support for specific candidates or policies, sustained interest about the administration and enforcement of campaign finance regulation does not exist. While public polls consistently indicate popular support for campaign finance reform, once put in context with other policy issues (i.e., national security, the economy, education, healthcare), this matter drops from a top policy priority for most citizens. This may mean that those involved in campaign finance reform activities are a select segment of the population because of their specialized knowledge, experience, and interest. This select group may or may not have the interest of the boarder community in mind when influencing public policy.

For the FEC, this may mean that as it attempts to implement and enforce campaign finance law, due to policy issue, scope, and interest, it is essentially dealing with a unique population that requires incumbent policy-makers to use a policy and administrative oversight that closely resembles a police-patrol oversight approach. Because those most interested in the policy probably occupy elite positions at the upper-end of the socioeconomic hierarchy in the United States, it is reasonable to conclude that the top-down policy-making process most realistically models campaign and election policy-making.

This is significant because this elite segment includes elected incumbent officials that support the agency through various annual resource allocations, or social and market elite that have access to these incumbent political officials. In either case, if this elite cadre has the institutional power to withhold and manipulate crucial administrative resources that the FEC needs to administer and enforce campaign finance regulation it can, in essence, make the difference between the organization meeting its legislatively delegated duties or not. Thus, agency policy implementation is not just an issue of administrative efficiency and effectiveness, but also one of survival. FEC decision-makers must balance the needs of effectively implementing promulgated public policy that safeguards the legitimacy of the campaign finance system and sustains democratic governance while avoiding actions that go against the desires of political officials and influential social interest.

The potential for policy outcomes that are inconsistent with democratic theory and government are therefore critical on two points. On the one hand, election policy is of great interest to incumbent political officials because despite reports of campaign finance regulation that does not work it is in their best interest to maintain the *status quo*. Why should incumbent politicians tamper with a campaign finance system that has and will continue to work in their interest, even at the possible expense of pluralist government? On the other hand, ramifications of campaign finance reform are so complex that periodic calls for change tend to focus mostly on short-term matters that quickly fade away by the next election cycle. In addition, policy overload among popular supporters quickly occurs and the issue disappears altogether from the top of government's policy agenda.

The one government administrative organization that attempts to fill this gap between narrow political intensity and public ignorance, the FEC, is structural and managerial linked it to hierarchical political officials in such a manner that institutional principals might inhibit dynamic regulatory administration and enforcement. Campaign finance policy is possibly the truest illustration of a specific public policy that is processed and implemented according to administrative arrangements that have the greatest potential for producing real and widespread undemocratic outcomes. One possible remedy for this potential problem is an informed electorate that is capable of overcoming policy issue complexity, scope, and interest barriers.

Conclusion

Developing a realistic and meaningful model of the policy-making process involves a careful consideration of policy complexity, scope, and interest. Because policy-making is a dynamic process that evolves over time, we need to understand the subtle manner in which specific policies and their implementation change in response to broader social and political features. This chapter illustrated that while most public policy may develop somewhere between a bottom-up and top-down model, there is at least one policy area that seems structurally best explained by a top-down model: election policy, specifically, campaign finance regulation. Because of this unique feature of campaign finance law, the administrative agency that enforces these regulation, the FEC, finds itself in a continual struggle to implement policy and avoid upsetting against political officials that support the agency in various ways. What role, however, might the electorate play in how political officials interact with FEC administration and enforcement of campaign finance regulation? The following chapter addresses the important issue of citizen knowledge of political information and its relationship to policy-making and policy implementation.

Chapter II

Political Knowledge & Policy Preferences

In the United States, the conventional view of democratic government is that the public is sovereign and therefore has a right to exercise its will through democratic elections. Specifically, that according to democratic theory and the practice of free and open elections citizens choose between competing candidates advocating a general policy agenda for government. However, some scholars contend that the electorates' limited knowledge of government, politics, and policy matters poses a significant threat to the stability and legitimacy of democratic government based on this popular notion (Pateman 1970; Zaller 1992). Research of electorate political knowledge indicates the public lacks fundamental information about basic government functions and important public policy issues. If the data support this accusation, this means the assumption that public policy based on informed public opinion is questionable.

This chapter looks at the issue of electorate political knowledge and its relationship to public policy. First, there is an overview data concerning electorate political knowledge and it is importance. Second, an examination of political preferences that highlights—in the absence of a knowledgeable electorate—how narrow political interests might develop and establish policy according to their needs. Third, there is a discussion of how political preference dominance of administrative structure and management arrangements shows how this might lead to undemocratic policy outcomes. This chapter illustrates the link between citizen knowledge about politics and government in the United States to the policy-making process. Understanding the link between political knowledge and public policy process helps us to better understand the administrative behavior of the FEC.

Political Knowledge of Government and Politics

Why is electorate knowledge of government important? The assumption is that an informed electorate that understands the structure, operation, and procedures of government and politics within a democracy can make informed decisions concerning available policy alternatives likely to advance their individual and collective goals. Unless the electorate attaches some political and communal value to promulgated public policies, they may not use electoral processes to influence political officials to serve their interests. Ideally, the electorate is able to choose between competing candidates and political party platforms to select the policy agenda consistent with their policy preferences. There is the expectation that a minimally knowledgeable electorate is aware of basic tradeoffs between alternative policies in cases where those tradeoffs would be obvious to the politically knowledgeable. In contrast, an uninformed electorate may not be able to link disparate political agendas with policy development implementation and outcomes.

This is usually the case concerning political responsibility for economic gains and loses. On the one hand, during times of economic prosperity, incumbent policy-makers are ready to claim their policy was responsible for spearheading an economic resurgence. On the other hand, during periods of economic recession, incumbent policy-makers quickly distance themselves, and their policies, from the decline. In either case, the electorate must be able to identify the importance of policy-makers and their actions regarding policy outcomes to properly assign credit or blame. While the United States may never have "responsible" government similar to that found in the British political system, American politicians, administrative officials, and political parties are nonetheless accountable to the electorate for their actions.

How Knowledgeable is the Electorate?

While the extent to which the electorate is uninformed about government and politics in the United States is disconcerting (as we will see in a moment), the significance of this situation necessitates viewing it in its proper perspective. Few would dispute the claim that the average citizen's knowledge about basic political information is not extensive. It is reasonable to conceive that (a) the public's political opinions lack detailed information and (b) that most citizens do not have a comprehensive awareness of current political and policy issues. This absence of a general awareness of basic information concerning contemporary issues might mean the electorates' ability to develop a collective policy picture to guide candidates for public office regarding a government policy agenda is limited. The absence of a collective understanding of basic political and policy issues, however, may provide well-organized special interest groups the opportunity they need to establish and implement a policy agenda and alternatives that benefit their own narrow policy goals (Zaller 1992: Delli Carpini and Keeter 1996.)

However, before condemning electorate ignorance we should try to understand that part of the problem might rest with the failure of public-opinion analysts to recognize and appreciate the extensive complexity and diversity of modern government and politics. The politically knowledgeable are individuals predisposed to this type of information due to their socioeconomic and ideological backgrounds that make it reasonable for them to bear the information cost for remaining up-to-date about government and political events. Those segments of society occupying leadership and decision-making positions in various public and private organizations and institutions recognize that it is their duty and responsibility to pay the information cost for remaining abreast of current political, governmental and policy events. Those segments of the society not occupying leadership or decision-making positions may find this information cost too high, and thus forego it. The following data, nonetheless, illustrates the extent of general electorate ignorance regarding knowledge of public affairs.

Two aspects of electorate knowledge deserve particular attention. First, over time a majority of the electorate simply does not know which of the two major political parties in the United States— Democrat or Republican—control Congress before an election (Table 2.1). Because a majority of the electorate does not know which of the two major political parties control Congress (or which chamber of the legislature) before an election, by extension, they are probably unclear about current public policy issues and debates. This suggests that because the electorate regularly does not know which party controls Congress before an election, it cannot accurately assign credit or blame for past policy outcomes to the responsible party. Without this informational capacity to properly assign policy outcome credit or blame to the responsible party in Congress, the accuracy of policy campaign and reporting are of little value. Thus, the gap between perceived responsibility and actual responsibility regarding policy outcomes in the United States may very well continue and possibly expand as political fortunes are made or lost according to these misperceptions (Campbell, Miller, and Converse 1980; Delli Carpini and Keeter 1996).

Table 2.1.   Electorate Knowledge of Control of Congress (pre-election)

Year	Incorrect / Do not know	Correct
1960	36%	64%
1964	36%	64%
1968	30%	70%
1972	36%	64%
1976	39%	61%
1980	29%	71%
1984	45%	55%
1988	41%	59%
1992	41%	59%
1996	27%	73%
2000	49%	51%

Source: *NES Table 1C.1 "Which Party Had Most Members of Congress Before the Election."*

Second, many individuals do not have a substantial ideological view of politics that allows them the ability to integrate multiple positions into a manageable framework to understand complex issues (Table 2.2). An interpretation of this information might lead to the conclusion that the average voter rarely shows the kind of ideological consistency evident in the well-informed voters that is important if ideology is used as an "information shortcut" for sorting competing political and policy agendas (Downs 1957; Campbell et al. 1960). This highlights the comparative inability of non-ideological voters to ideological voters to identify linkages among and across policy issues. The assumption is that an ideologically aware electorate can detect contradictory policies and take corrective action.

Table 2.2.   Political Ideology of the Electorate

Year	Liberal		Moderate		Conservative	DK
1972	8%	10%	27%	15%	11%	28%
1976	8%	8%	25%	12%	13%	33%
1980	8%	9%	20%	13%	15%	36%
1984	9%	9%	23%	14%	15%	30%
1988	8%	9%	22%	15%	17%	30%
1992	10%	10%	23%	15%	16%	27%
1996	8%	10%	24%	15%	18%	25%
2000	11%	9%	23%	12%	18%	27%

Source: *NES Table 3.1 "Liberal-Conservative Self-Identification."*

In addition, the electorate's lack of knowledge about basic political and ideological interconnections between and across policy issues may cast further doubt on the conventional wisdom that contends popular opinion—based on voter knowledge—is a significant determinant of public policy. Without knowledge of the basic rules of politics and a well-grounded ideological position, the interconnections between public policies not only become meaningless but also fail to register among the electorate as important. Thus, the electorate cannot link various policy objectives to make election decisions that enhance their condition (Zaller 1992; Delli Carpini and Keeter 1996). Table 2.3 presents data indicating the level of trust and efficacy in government decreases over time. This decline may be due, in part, to an electorate that is neither politically knowledgeable nor ideologically driven.

Table 2.3.   Trust in Government and Political Efficacy

Year	Trust in Government	External Political Efficacy
1960	0%	74%
1964	52%	67%
1968	45%	57%
1972	38%	55%
1976	30%	52%
1980	27%	53%
1984	38%	63%
1988	34%	49%
1992	29%	51%
1996	32%	38%
2000	36%	46%

Source: *NES Table 5A.5 "Trust in Government Index" & Table 5B.4 "External Political Efficacy Index."*

How Much Information is Necessary?

What should voters know to exercise significant democratic influence over government policy? There are three minimal knowledge prerequisites for voters to be able to exert meaningful influence over government. First, voters must be aware of current issues. Second, they must have a position on the issues. Third, they must know candidates' positions on relevant issues. While these are not sufficient prerequisites for control over public policy, a minimally informed electorate is necessary to at the very least begin to have a substantive understanding of which of the available policy agendas presented to them by candidates running for public office are most likely to help advance their own individual and collective goals. Ultimately, however, there is no correct response to the question of how much information is enough.

Despite these dismal findings regarding electorate knowledge, perhaps this is the wrong question. Instead of questioning *what* the electorate should know about politics, maybe we should focus attention on the question of *how much* knowledge of modern democratic government and politics is reasonable. Low levels of electorate knowledge of government and politics might be due to the overwhelming and ever increasing number of policy issues and political complexities. If this is the case, then perhaps it is unreasonable to expect the average voters to comprehend the scope and size contemporary public affairs. Modern government and politics are difficult even for the well informed. Keeping track of current and developing events is simply daunting. It may therefore reasonable to assume that even the knowledgeable segment of the electorate have difficulty understanding the complexities regarding a modernizing large-scale democracy such as the United States. Table 2.4 presents data supporting this position by indicating that over time the electorate view government and politics as "too complex" for them to understand. How do groups interested in government policy-making reduce the level of uncertainty that is inevitable due to incomplete information caused by the complexity of modern government?

Table 2.4.   Electorate View of "Complex Government"

Year	Agree	Disagree	Neither	Don't Know
1952	71%	28%	--	1
1956	64%	36%	--	0
1960	59%	41%	--	0
1964	67%	32%	--	1
1968	71%	29%	--	0
1972	74%	26%	--	0
1976	71%	27%	--	2
1980	70%	28%	--	2
1984	71%	29%	--	0
1988	70%	21%	8%	0
1992	66%	27%	7%	0
1996	63%	27%	10%	0
2000	60%	32%	7%	0

Source: *NES Table 5B.1 "Politics is Too Complicated."*

Political Preference of Administrative Arrangements

Political uncertainty has a profound affect on the decision-making of officeholders, administrative officials, and special interest groups. In particular, each of these factions know that current policies and administrative arrangements which provide beneficial returns are subject to change by future officeholders that might have a different set of policy and political goals. Therefore, incumbent policy-makers must develop and institute rules and procedures that maintain stable returns in the face of an uncertain future policy and political climate.

The literature notes development of economic-based agency theory that features relationships between principals and agents in the area of regulatory administration that address the issue of how to deal with future uncertainty (Moe 1984; Wood and Waterman 1993; Gerber and Teske 2000). The application of agency theory to the study of political-administrative relationships assume (a) hierarchical relationships; (b) political-administrative interests diverge over time; and (c) elected officials try to influence implementation. (See Worsham, Eisner, and Ringquist (1997) for a discussion of agency theory.) The key issue is how elected officeholders having legitimate hierarchical power over administrative officials overcome problems associated with agency policy development and implementation that might be inconsistent with legislative policy desires.

Elected officials can overcome these problems due to their ability to determine administrative arrangements—agency hierarchy and enforcement style. Because elected officials determine the administrative arrangement of regulatory agencies that enforce public policies these officials can keep administrative behavior within predetermined boundaries. By structuring administrative decision-making hierarchy and enforcement style *ex ante*, elected officials establish the "rules of the game" by which regulatory agencies administer and enforce the law. In addition, legislative design of the "rule of the game" may enfranchise or exclude certain groups from participating in a particular regulatory industry (Tullock 1989; North 1990). Thus, by instituting certain administrative arrangements, legislators may reduce uncertainty, limit "bureaucratic drift," and enfranchise (or disenfranchise) select groups (Weingast and Moran 1983; McCubbins, Noll, and Weingast 1989; Horn 1995).

Comparing how economic and political organizations address uncertainty provides a meaningful explanation of how political interests use administrative arrangements to reduce uncertainty (Moe 1995). An explanation of how an economic organization addresses the issue of uncertainty focuses on transaction costs and asset specificity based on property rights. In this context, economic organizations concern themselves with the technical task of putting their property to its best use. Economic organizations do not need to have identical interest to agree on rules governing their relationships. Economic organizations only need to agree on a set of arrangements that benefit all parties and allow for the rejections of certain arrangements. Compromise, for economic organizations, allows individuals with conflicting interests to create arrangements that are *Pareto optimal* (Williamson and Winter 1993).

Terry Moe (1995) provides an explanation of how a political organization addresses the issue of uncertainty that focuses on the task of instituting administrative arrangements that can protect their interest over time from present and future political opponents. In politics, compromise means something different in comparison to what compromise means for economic organizations. Developing and instituting administrative arrangements, for political organizations, is a process in which incumbent public authority imposes their institutional outcomes on everyone else. Political interests not having majority control face the possibility that those in the majority might establish new arrangements that place them in a worse-off position. The reasons for compromise between majority and minority political interests are different from those we expect in voluntary exchanges among economic interests. While economic interests have something to exchange that is of some mutual benefit to involved parties (i.e., property), political actors, lacking the equivalent, place those out-of-power in the position of having additional costs imposed upon them. Political actors have the opportunity to create administrative arrangements that are effective and efficient, but also coercive. Thus, the nature of political compromise, under a climate of coercion, is to create administrative arrangements that produce sub-*Pareto optimal* policy outcomes (Moe 1995).

This occurs because the American separation of power system facilitates some degree of compromise. Political compromise means granting the losing side concessions concerning administrative arrangements that the losing party might initially oppose. However, allowing the minority the concession of involvement in determining administrative arrangements, administrative feature begin to overburden public organizations. The result of this additional "layering" is increasing ineffectiveness and inefficiency. These political choices about administrative arrangements have important consequences for policy implementation and outcomes (Light 1995; Moe 1995).

Political choices about administrative arrangements are implicitly choices about politics and policy. Just as political compromise can weaken policy during its development it can also weaken administrative structure and management. This produces administrative arrangements that are less policy oriented and more politically oriented. Administrative structure and management, consequently, have a fundamental design flaw: the arrangements ensure that achieving effective and efficient policy outcomes are difficult (Moe 1995). Because a conflict exists between the goals and aspirations of the administrators and political preferences, the problem of implementing policy consistent with political desires and the tenets of democratic theory are difficult. Implementation of public policy may not take place or may produce policy outcomes inconsistent with the underlying goals of democratic government. What problems might this pose for administrators?

The problem is of two types: *shirking* and *slippage*. Shirking is the result of a conflict of goals between the political principal and administrative agent. The agent may pursue its own objectives to the detriment of the principal's interests: agent policy selection might differ from that preferred by the principal. In addition, information asymmetries between principal and agent exacerbate faulty administrative arrangements. Slippage denotes problems of design and operation. Different institutional designs for agency decision-making will lead to different outcomes chosen by the agent. It may not be possible to create administrative arrangements that perfectly translate the intentions of multiple and diverse political principals into cohesive administrative agent action. All things being equal, shirking and slippage might tend to exacerbate already flawed administrative arrangements designed to produce sub-*Pareto optimal* policy outcomes. Thus, political officials prefer to structure decision-making processes to overcome this uncertainty and establish stable organizational decision-making. Political officials attempt to influence administrative behavior using institutional power to create structural and managerial arrangements that reduce political uncertainty and bureaucratic drift.

Structural Arrangements

Structural arrangements seek to solve problems associated with political uncertainty and bureaucratic drift by constraining the discretion of agency decision-makers, thus channeling decision-making toward alternatives that comply with the intent of institutional principals. The substantive discretion of any government agency consists of various policy alternatives from which the organization may select one or more alternatives individually or in combination. Several structural factors, in part, influence organizational decision-making in the public sector. First, *institutional setting* looks at organizational decision-making discretion within its distinctive institutional context (e.g., board or commission). Second, *regulatory scope* addresses the question of what methods are available to an organization to do its job (e.g., civil or criminal enforcement). Third, *regulatory instruments* focus on the tools available to an organization for meeting its delegated duties (e.g., command and control). Fourth, *procedural requirements* are those predetermined activities that require an organization to participate in specific activities on an annual, biannual, or special event timetable (e.g., appropriation hearings or convening of special investigative committees). Individually and collectively, these structural arrangements serve to reduce agent discretion and channel organizational decision-making processes toward predictable alternatives.

Management Arrangements

Management arrangements seek to influence administrative behavior in such a manner that agency actions, over time, remain consistent with the interests of its institutional principals. Political officials, when establishing and developing a relationship with an administrative agency, will attempt to induce agency compliance through the application of an intricate system of management *rewards* and *sanctions*. An example of a reward might be legislators agreeing to an agency request for additional staffing to handle a growing workload. An example of a sanction might include not only the rejection of a staff increase request, but also the thickening of administrative procedures by expanding the organization's responsibilities and duties that put greater pressure on already strained resources. These management rewards and sanctions arise largely through the exercise of the principal's constitutionally defined powers of appropriation, legislation, appointment, and jurisdiction.

In general, political officials have all the powers they needs to ensure agency compliance. Further, although sanctions might only be used infrequently, their presence creates incentives for organization decision-makers to comply with political desires. Political officials hold the power of life or death over most government agencies by threat of termination. Political officials, for instance, can carryout this threat by either refusal to renew appropriation, legislative power, appointment ability, specifying the jurisdiction resources, or through the combined use of any or all of these powers. For the FEC, this means that Congress, the president, and the Supreme Court can directly or indirectly influence what actions the agency does or does not conduct regarding the administration and enforcement of campaign finance law.

The FEC and Regulation of Campaign Finances

The FEC has the responsibility and duty of ensuring that those involved in legislative and presidential campaigns adhere to regulations concerning the conduct of federal campaigns and elections. How does our view of the FEC change once we realize that those involved in legislative and presidential campaigns, in addition, participate in determining FEC administrative arrangements? It is reasonable to consider that these political interests might try to establish FEC administrative arrangements that benefit their political and policy objectives at the possible cost of the broader society by jeopardizing the integrity of the campaign and election system?

During the early 1970's, the Watergate affair and other investigations disgraced both Republicans and Democrats. Republicans were guilty of wiretapping, paying burglars with laundered money from Nixon's reelection committee, illegal corporate campaign donations to Nixon's campaign, selling ambassadorships, and using hush money to finance cover-ups. Democrats were guilty of illegal donations to the campaigns of Democratic candidates. This included the 1972 presidential primary campaign of Hubert Humphrey and Wilbur Mills. Fallout from such extensive corruption of the campaign finance system forced Congress to seriously consider establishing an independent regulatory agency to administrate and enforce recently established campaign finance regulation.

By early 1973, the 93rd Congress began discussions about alternative administrative arrangements for the proposed new federal regulatory agency to administrate and enforcement the campaign finance system. These discussions occur primarily along political and ideological lines with debate about agency structure focusing on the possible size of the appointed commission. Included in this debate is the question of whether the chair of the proposed regulatory agency should have a broad range of power to facilitate strong agency leadership or limited power resulting in weak agency leadership. There is also the question of commissioners' length of service and what, if any, limits should be instituted concerning re-appointment for future regulators to the administrative agency. Structural considerations during this formulation period generally sought to establish a simple and transparent administrative agency. Issues relating to administrative arrangements are: (a) Should the agency have a multiple year or annual budget?; (b) To what extent should the agency have power to establish legislation on its own?; (c) Who should be appointed to the agency and what, if any, restrictions should there be on such appointees?; and (d) Should the proposed regulatory agency be limited in its capacity to represent itself in court? Overall, administrative structure and management considerations establish organizational procedures that link the proposed regulatory agency close to political interests.

By the end of 1974, Congress arrived at a compromise between legislators wanting an expansive regulatory presence and those desiring a limited regulatory presence regarding the implementation and enforcement of campaign finance law. In the end, legislators amended the FECA and established a politically balanced six-member commission, two appointed by the president, and the other four appointed by congressional leadership. The House Clerk and the Senate Secretary would serve on the commission as *ex officio* members. Instead of a permanent chair, leadership of the commission would rotate among the six commissioners, each serving in turn for only one year with limited power. The chair would preside at meetings, sign correspondence, and exert perhaps a small influence over internal procedures and the agenda. Such a weak leadership position ensures the ineffectiveness of the agency from the start.

Because of the Supreme Court's decision in *Buckley v. Valeo* (1976) provisions allowing solely for congressional appointments to the FEC are ruled an unconstitutional encroachment on executive power. Following the Court's ruling Congress restructured and revived the FEC, but required four of the six commissioners to vote affirmatively for commission action. The agency retains the Secretary of the Senate and the Clerk of the House as *ex officio* commission members and Congress established new guidelines concerning submission of allegations, implementation of a conciliatory enforcement model, and retaining presidential appointment of commissioners.

While these matters lead to some administrative resolution, the overarching issue regarding the legitimacy of the federal campaign finance system remained unsettled. Eventually, as the electorate grows increasingly bewildered by the complexities of modern government, money in politics takes on greater importance. A primary concern of reformist was that policy preferences of elite stakeholders might dominant the policy agendas of lawmakers, thereby leading to a situation in which government policy-making and implementation produce outcomes inconsistent with the tenets of democratic theory. Because this fiscal "arms race" could make government less responsive to the needs of a broader society, according to reform advocates, we run the risk of developing what Mancur Olson refers to as "institutional sclerosis" (Olson 1982). This fear developed out of an extensive campaign finance history that illustrates creative attempts to use money to determine election outcomes.

Conclusion

To assess electoral knowledge of government actions and what this means to political-administrative relationships involving policy implementation, this chapter provided an overview data concerning electorate political knowledge and it is an important indicator that the electorate lacks fundamental information about government, politics, and policy issue. This chapter, in addition, indicated that in the absence of an informed electorate, narrow political interests might develop an establish government policy according to their needs, thereby biasing the policy-making process toward a top-down model. This skewing of the policy-making process might lead to undemocratic policy outcomes. While this chapter properly positioned public knowledge in relation to the policy-making process, a closer examination of the historic roots of government regulation of money in politics is necessary to appreciate the social and political context of this election administration and regulation.

Chapter III

A Brief History of Campaign Finance Regulation

The issue of money in federal elections becomes more intense as events such as Watergate and questions about foreign contributions in federal elections propel this topic toward the forefront of contemporary political discourse (Malbin 1984; Sabato and Simpson 1996). Along with this increasing public criticism of campaign financing in the United States, additional criticism focuses on the Federal Election Commission (FEC). Of primary interest concerning regulation of campaign financing in federal elections are questions about if and how the relationship between political officials and the FEC determines the agency's ability to investigate possible violations of the election law (Oldaker 1986; Hamilton 1994). If political officials have the ability to influence FEC administrative behavior, what might this mean regarding implementation of election law that work toward the benefit of the many and not just the few?

This chapter provides an overview of efforts to regulate money in politics. First, there is a brief discussion about the importance of election policy to democratic government. Second, there is a review of historical issues concerning the increasing use of money in federal elections and government efforts to control its corrosive effects over time. Third, there is a discussion of contemporary issues regarding the regulation of campaign finances in federal elections and what these new methods of paying for campaigns may mean for campaign and election outcomes.

Election Policy

Election policy is fundamentally political. What is at stake in a democracy such as the United States in an election is the distribution of political and policy-making power (Kingdon 1984; Katz 1994). The basic values at issue in competitive elections are the foundation of a free and democratic society. Thus, the ramifications of election policy formation, administration, and enforcement extend to all areas of society through their implementation by government agencies (Renstrom and Rogers 1989; Renstrom 1991).

A serious dilemma concerning the enforcement of campaign finance law arises, however, when we realize that those who determine these laws are also subject to punishment according to these statutes. On the one hand, election policy is too important and sensitive a matter for elected officials not to play a significant role in its creation and enforcement. On the other hand, it is reasonable to question the assumption that elected officials can create and develop a regulatory system that does not in some manner provide them, and their related interests, with additional benefit (Danziger and Gottschalk 1995). This is a question more about unquantifiable *degrees* of benefit rather than quantifiable *absolute* benefit.

As a public policy area, election policy has two distinct approaches. First, election policy focuses on the central role of democratic elections providing government with institutional leadership. Although democratic values and procedures are indispensable to democratic society, leadership is necessary for stable government. Second, election policy focuses on the issue of how a particular policy decision may affect other public policies. For instance, amending election rules may favor certain candidates or interests over others in competitive elections. This might therefore lead to the development of campaign and election policy skewed toward the advantage or disadvantage of a particular political candidate, ideology, or interest (Mayhew 1974). Consequently, while it is important to note the distinctions between policy leadership and policy implementation, their interrelationship is unavoidable.

Beyond issues concerning institutional leadership and policy processes, analysis of election policy also reveals the conflict between regulation of campaign finances and the principle of free speech (Smolla 1992). Advocates of federally funded elections, such as Common Cause and the Center for Public Integrity, contend that the right to free political speech is meaningless unless one also has the means of disseminating political ideas and opinions among the community. Regardless, advocates of a free-market approach to federal campaign finance policy, such as the Brookings Institution and the American Enterprise

Institute, contend that restricting the right to spend money for disseminating political ideas and opinions is effectively restricting free speech. Those opposing this free-market approach counter that unlimited spending in election campaigns affords a disproportionate amount of freedom of speech to those with greater financial resources (Sabato 1989; Austin-Smith 1993; Matthews 1994; Allen and Jensen 1995). At this point, it becomes clear that the cleavage between the regulatory and free-market approaches to federal campaign finance policy is real and significant. Attention therefore shifts to the development of mechanisms for resolving this conflict.

In the United States, federal election policy attempts to achieve effective freedom of speech that equalizes access to the means of disseminating political ideas in a manner that does not provide a disproportional advantage to any particular political interest, group, or organization. This type of policy approach, nonetheless, raises questions concerning to whom does the limitation apply and the definition of expenditure. In addition, there is the issue of restricting the source and amount of contributions in competitive contests for public office (Glantz, Abramowitz, and Burkart 1976; Arneson 1982). The point is that election policy is not only a difficult theoretical issue concerning free speech rights, but it also involves challenging practical issues such as policy administration and implementation. The following sections review important historical and contemporary issues relating to this matter that is necessary to understand to conduct a systematic analysis how the FEC's relationship with political officials influences its administrative behavior.

Classic Issues

The history of campaign finance regulation in the United States is a long and complex tale of government's attempt to prevent the corrupting influence of money in politics in order to maintain the legitimacy of the campaign and election system (Heidenheimer 1970; Ferguson 1995; Hibbing and Welch 1997). Over the years, the nature and complexity of money in politics has changed incrementally. Federal campaign finance law during the pre-World War II period sought primarily to address what most individuals might commonly refer to as traditional abuses of money in politics (i.e., cash bribes, unreported contributions, and graft). However, following this period of traditional campaign finance abuse, the post-World War II period is characterized by more complex and strategic uses of money that seek to provide specific interests campaign and electoral advantage. This evolutionary development manifests itself today in the form of modern political corruption that deals less with direct cash bribes or payoffs and more with exploitation of elaborate legal loopholes and financial transactions. Thus, the following sections provide a brief, but insightful review of the history of campaign finance corruption and government efforts to regulate the use of money in federal campaigns and elections in the United States to illustrate these developments. Please note that the division of this information into pre-World War II and post-World War II periods is for literary convenience mainly and may not precisely represent historical paradigm shifts.

Pre-World War II Period

Although popular debate concerning the use of money in political campaigns began in 1791 with disputes over campaign expenditures during Alexander Hamilton's presidential campaign, it was not until 1832 that the topic became a substantive policy issue. President Andrew Jackson's threat not to renew the Bank of the United States charter provided Henry Clay, who supported bank charter renewal, a platform from which to solicit large amounts of campaign funds. Jackson, regardless, won re-election in part by portraying the Bank and its supporters as degrading the integrity of the political process by using excessive contributions to support of Clay (Thayer 1973). Although the actual dollar amount in this case was not the determining factor in Jackson's victory, the issue of money in politics began to filter into the public and political campaign and election discourse.

The late 1800's provide useful examples of early government efforts to address the problem of money in politics by responding to reports of government employee involvement in campaign financing activities. First, in 1867 there was a provision in a naval appropriations bill that made it illegal for a naval officer or government employee to request political contributions from workmen in Navy yards. Second, responding to public outrage over the assassination of President James Garfield in 1881 by an embittered attorney who sought a government post, Chester Arthur, who succeeded to the Presidency, pushed for the enactment of the Pendleton Act of 1883. The Pendleton Act of 1883 established a bipartisan Civil Service Commission that prevented incumbent officeholders from using the spoils system to their political advantage and prohibited civil service employees from soliciting political contributions (Adamany 1972).

During this period, referred to as the Gilded Age, not only did great economic gaps between the rich and poor develop, but the use of money to improperly influence political campaigns and elections expanded as allegations of political corruption at all levels of government became increasingly common. At the local level, colorful figures such as Boss Tweed in New York, "Bathhouse John" Coughlin in Chicago, the "Old Regulars" in New Orleans, and A. A. "Doc" Ames in Minneapolis developed political machines to decide election winners and losers. At the federal level before the Arthur administration, President Ulysses S. Grant's administration was associated with such infamous scandals such as the Gold Conspiracy, the Whiskey Ring, and the Salary Club. These overt and obvious uses of money to buy political influence ultimately galvanized public sentiment to advocate reform of the campaign finance system (Thayer 1973).

Following these public indiscretions at the turn of the century, Progressive Era advocates began the first coordinated effort to systematically regulate money in politics. By 1900, Progressive reformers reported that the excessive contributions by wealthy business interests had become the primary source for political fundraising. These Progressive politicians and groups charged that the wealthy donors were corrupting government and the election process by gaining special privileges due to their large campaign contributions. Even so, Progressive efforts to establish comprehensive campaign finance reform were unsuccessful until the 1904 presidential controversy.

In 1904, Democratic presidential nominee Judge Alton Parker proclaimed that business interests were purchasing executive influence by contributing large sums of money to President Theodore Roosevelt's election campaign. Although President Roosevelt denied the charge, investigations following the election indicated that several major businesses did make large contributions to the Republican campaign in support of Roosevelt's reelection campaign. In response to this controversy, President Roosevelt advocated for campaign finances reforms that ultimately lead to the creation of the National Publicity Law Organization, a citizens group that lobbied for vigorous regulation of campaign contributions. Although the National Publicity Law Organization's efforts did not result in the enactment of what some might consider substantial campaign finance reforms, the group did bring greater political and public attention to the issue (Corrado, Mann, Ortiz, Potter, and Sorauf 1997).

By 1907, Congress did enact legislation to regulate corporate and banking contributions in federal elections. Congressman Benjamin Tillman (D-SC) led this legislative effort by supporting a bill that restricted corporate contributions in federal elections. Popularly known as the Tillman Act, this law prohibited corporate and banking interests from contributing to federal political campaigns. Following passage of the Tillman Act, however, political and social pressure grew to enact additional legislation to prevent the harmful influence of money in politics.

In 1910, the Republican majority in Congress passed legislation that required national political party committees to report any contributions or expenditures made regarding campaigns for the House of Representatives. The Federal Corrupt Practices Act required national party committees conducting business in two or more states to send post-election receipt and expenditure reports to the Clerk of the House of Representatives for review. However, because this Act only affected the national party committees and their congressional campaign committees, and did not require any disclosure before an election, advocates for campaign finance reform pushed for additional regulation.

Continuation of these campaign finance reforms led to the 1911 Federal Corrupt Practices Act Amendments that established detailed disclosure requirements and spending limits for federal campaigns. The 1911 Federal Corrupt Practices Act Amendments also extended disclosure rules by requiring members of Congress to report all financial activities and that campaign committees report their finances both before and after an election. Following the start of World War I in 1914 and America's subsequent participation in 1917, however, a political movement developed to undo previous campaign finance reforms.

For example, in 1918 when Republican Truman Newberry defeated Democratic Henry Ford for the U.S. Senate from Michigan, Ford charged that Newberry exceeded the $10,000 limit in primary elections to secure the Republican nomination. Newberry, convicted of violating the 1911 Tillman Act Amendments, challenged this decision before the U.S. Supreme Court. The Supreme Court implied in *Newberry v. United States* (1921) that the congressional authority to regulate elections did not extend to the party primaries and nomination activities and questioned the congressional right to regulate nominations. Although this commonly held finding from *Newberry* was later overturned in *United States v. Classic* (1941), it became clear that establishing strict campaign finance regulatory methods would not be easy (Corrado, Mann, Ortiz, Potter, and Sorauf 1997). Even so, there was progress in this area.

The 1925 Federal Corrupt Practices Act Amendments strengthened existing disclosure requirements and increased expenditure limits. These Amendments to the Federal Corrupt Practices Act were similar to earlier legislation in that the amendments did not substantively change federal campaign finance law, but revised disclosure rules to prevent illegal financial activity characteristic of the Teapot Dome scandal. These new amendments required all multi-state political committees to file quarterly reports that included all contributions over $100, even in non-election years (Overacker 1932). Effective campaign finance administration, nonetheless, remained essentially limited at best.

Though the Federal Corrupt Practices Act established clear reporting requirements, it did not provide enforcement mechanisms necessary for meaningful federal campaign regulation, administration, and when necessary, enforcement. None of the federal laws concerning campaign finance regulation, however, specified who has access to campaign committee reports, their public publication, or reporting format. Because the destruction of these documents occurred after two years, accessing this information through the Clerk of the House or Secretary of the Senate is difficult if not impossible (Thayer 1973). Despite widespread knowledge of noncompliance with existing federal campaign finance law, in the context of government efforts to deal with Depression Era problems, Congress did not again address campaign finance reform seriously until the establishment of President Franklin Roosevelt's New Deal policies.

Beginning in 1939, opponents of President Roosevelt's liberal public polices become wary of the prospect that an expanding federal workforce created by the New Deal might become a permanent Democratic political force. In their attempt to minimize this possibility, Congress passed the Hatch Act of 1939 to limit federal employee involvement in campaign and election activities. The Hatch Act also extended prohibitions on federal employees in federal elections first established in the Pendleton Act of 1883 and related judicial decisions. The Hatch Act, and subsequent amendments, asserted the right of Congress to regulate primary elections (including provisions limiting contributions and expenditures in congressional elections) and prohibited political activity by federal workers not restricted by the Pendleton Act. In addition, following the United States military efforts in World War II, the Taft-Hartley Act of 1947 was enacted prohibiting labor and corporate organization expenditures and contributions in federal elections.

Collectively, the Pendleton Act, Tillman Act, Publicity Act, Federal Corrupt Practices Act, Hatch Act, and Taft-Hartley Act (a) limited contributions (b) prevented certain sources of funds (c) controlled campaign spending and (d) required public disclosure of campaign finances. However, while federal reforms had begun to address traditional sources of political corruption by the end of the World War II period, collectively these efforts failed to establish administrative responsibility for regulating and enforcing the campaign finance regulation. Progressive Era campaign finance reforms could not and did not begin to address the complex political and legal questions that would come to characterize post-World War II American politics. With this new era of campaign financing, those interested in reducing the corrupting effect of money in politics must rethink fundamental constitutional issues.

Post World War II Period

As industrial, commercial and social activity increased following World War II, new concerns regarding the conduct of federal campaigns and elections also emerged. Essentially, while party organizations remained important sources of revenue, the way campaign administration began to focus more on individual candidates and less on the political parties (Aldrich 1995). Candidates for federal office in this post-World War II period began establishing their own committees and raised funds independent of party organizations. This fragmentation of the campaign and election system, along with greater use of media and professional campaign specialists, led to an increasing need for more money (Alexander 1980). Yet, despite increasing anxiety about the rising cost of campaigning Congress was slow to act. The only serious political gesture made toward campaign finance reform by Congress between World War II and the early 1960s was President John F. Kennedy's decision to create the Commission on Campaign Costs in 1962 to develop related legislation. Regardless, the Commission dissolved shortly after Kennedy's assassination without having any of its policy recommendations enacted (Thayer 1973).

Despite past failures to enact substantive federal campaign finance reform, Congress did move forward. Congress passed major campaign finance reform that reduced the influence of wealthy donors and eased the fundraising demands in presidential campaigns through public subsidies to political parties. Subsidies for this presidential election campaign fund would allow taxpayers to use a federal tax check-off to give a small dollar amount to finance this program. Although Congress passed this income tax check-off bill as part of the 1971 Revenue Act, partisan debate forced a change in its effective date due to concerns regarding the upcoming 1972 Nixon-McGovern presidential campaign. On the one hand, the Democratic Party, which was $9 million in debt following the 1968 presidential election, said the voluntary plan was necessary to counter the influence of wealthy campaign contributors. On the other hand, the Republican Party, which was financially solvent, contended that the public funding plan was a device to rescue the

Democratic Party from financial difficulty. President Richard Nixon did ultimately sign this legislation into law but had its effective date changed from 1972 to 1976 (Congressional Quarterly 1982).

These efforts, nonetheless, failed to address what continued to be a major problem plaguing the American campaign and election system: effective regulatory administration and enforcement of the campaign finance law. This shortcoming was obvious during the 1960's and early 1970's. Numerous reports of campaign finance irregularities regarding the failure to provide required activity reports and exceeding set spending limits established by earlier legislation began to make news headlines (Adamany and Agree 1975). Fueling this growing anxiety about money in politics was the escalating costs of campaigns and elections. For instance, from 1952 to 1968, total campaign spending in presidential elections (inflation adjusted) doubled from approximately $140 million to $300 million (Alexander 1980). Therefore, members of Congress fearing the prospect of having to raise increasing amounts of money enacted legislation to control campaign costs (McCarthy 1972; Alexander 1971, 1972, 1976; Peabody and Berry 1972; Berry and Goldman 1973; Benson 1978).

In response to these reports of campaign and election corruption, Congress passed the 1971 Federal Election Campaign Act (FECA) and a new era in campaign financing began. In general, the FECA did curb the rising costs of campaigns and strengthened reporting and disclosure requirements. The first part of FECA established contribution limits on the amount a candidate could give to his or her own campaign and set ceilings on the amount a campaign could spend on media advertising. The second part of FECA imposed strict public disclosure procedures on federal candidates and political committees (Alexander 1976).

Congressional amendments to FECA in 1974 responded further to public pressure for additional reform in the wake of the Watergate scandal and other reports of campaign finance abuse related to the 1972 Nixon re-election effort. Investigations into Nixon's re-election campaign revealed extensive use of illegal contributions and undisclosed funds. Based on this evidence Congress amended the FECA in 1974 adopting stricter limits on campaign contributions and expenditures, but also establishing the FEC as the regulatory agency in charge of campaign finance administration and enforcement (Adamany and Agree 1975). However, while many applauded these reforms, others questioned the constitutionality of these measures. Objections to the 1974 FECA Amendments are summarized in Senator James Buckley (Conservative Party-NY) and Eugene McCarthy's (D-MN) lawsuit against the Secretary of the Senate Francis Valeo.

In *Buckley v. Valeo* (1976), the Supreme Court upheld FECA Amendment's contribution limits because these limits served the government's interest in safeguarding the integrity of elections by preventing the appearance of corruption (Barnum 1985). However, the Court overturned the Amendment's expenditure limits, stating that a fundamental effect of these limitations was to restrict the quantity of campaign speech, and therefore, infringe upon constitutional freedoms (Sorauf 1992). Thus, the Court found the 1974 FECA Amendment's expenditure limits imposed more severe restrictions on freedoms of political expression and relationship than did contribution limits (Bauer and Kafka 1984; Gross 1991). The Court however did note that expenditure limits placed on publicly funded candidates were constitutional because candidates for president were not obligated to accept matching funds and affirmed this later finding in the *Republican National Committee v. FEC* (1980). In addition, the Court maintained other public funding provisions and upheld disclose and record-keeping requirements. Finally, the Court found that the method of appointing FEC Commissioners violated the constitutional principle of separation of powers, since Congress, not the President, appointed four of the six Commissioners who would exercise executive powers (Sorauf 1992).

In response to the findings in *Buckley v. Valeo*, the 1976 FECA Amendments required that the President appoint all six Commissioners, with confirmation by the Senate. Accordingly, the Commission reconstituted as President Gerald Ford appointed and the Senate confirmed all six Commissioners. In addition, the 1976 Amendments attempted to clarify ambiguous guidelines stated in an earlier FEC Advisory Opinion (AO 1975-23) concerning corporate solicitation of employees and stockholders. The FECA Amendments, additionally, encouraged state and local party activity and increased the public funding grants for presidential nominating conventions (Bozeman, Reed, and Scott 1992; Brown, Powell, and Wilcox 1995).

Since 1979, Congress has amended the FECA several times. These amendments include simplification of campaign reporting procedures, repeal of the grandfather clause that permitted Congressmen to convert excess campaign funds to personal use, and more funding for national nominating conventions (Alexander and Bauer 1991). In addition, Congress enacted legislation assigning significant new administrative duties to the FEC under the National Voter Registration Act of 1993 (P.L. 103-31) and increased the tax check-off for the Presidential Election Campaign Fund (*FEC 20 Year Report, April 1995*). Despite these legislative efforts to regulate money in politics, new and more complex issues plague the campaign finance system. The following section is a brief overview of contemporary issues that influence public opinion to believe the problem of money in politics remains as serious as ever.

Contemporary Issues

While conventional wisdom contends that the current federal campaign finance system prevents traditional forms of political corruption, reform advocates believe modern political corruption continues through influence peddling and the exploitation of legal loopholes. Reform advocates assert these new forms of corruption are more insidious than outright bribery because of they are institutionalized. Table 3.1 provides data that show the extent to which political party fundraising had increased from 1983 to 1996. The data illustrates not only the rise in political fundraising over time, but also underscores the increasing ability of political parties to raise campaign funds in presidential and congressional elections. Hall and Wayman (1990) note in their classic study of money in politics that campaign contributions do not necessarily buy votes but instead use campaign contributions as a tool for purchasing *access* to legislators and their staff to mobilize or demobilize congressional committees.

Table 3.1.   Political Party Fundraising, 1983-2000

Year	Amount Raised (millions)				
	1983-84	1987-88	1991-92	1995-96	1999-00
Dem	$98.5	$127.9	$177.7	$221.6	$275.2
Rep	$297.9	$263.3	$267.3	$416.5	$465.8

Source: Federal Election Commission. (2000). *FEC Reports Increase In Party Fundraising For 2000* [Online]. Available: http://www.fec.gov/press/press2001/051501partyfund.html. [2001, December 5].

A primary concern with present efforts to administer and enforce the federal campaign finance law is that the FEC is unable to keep pace with an increasing regulatory workload. In a recent review of the agency's operations, Pricewaterhouse Coopers noted that the FEC suffers from numerous administrative and resource inefficiencies. First, FEC campaign finance reports disclosure and review activities rely on an antiquated paper-based and manual transaction coding, entry, verification, and clarification process. Second, FEC organizational units operate in a compartmentalized and autonomous manner that leads to poor communication, collaboration, and lack of innovation. Third, because of limited resources and increasing case complexity, the workload of the FEC exceeds its effective capacity (Pricewaterhouse Coopers, 1999). FEC Commissioners themselves state consistently the agency needs a larger workforce to keep pace with its workload (*FEC Annual Reporst, 1986-1999*).

Further, some reform advocates contend Congress handicaps FEC ability to enforce the law by mandating that a pre-determined portion of the agency's budget go toward specific non-enforcement related projects, instead of increasing an already overburdened staff. (Note: A number of organizations, such as Common Cause, the Brookings Institution, and the Washington Post, have online sites that provide helpful commentary and data concerning FEC inability to accomplish its regulatory duties in an effective and efficient manner.) A report issued by the CATO Institute notes that if congressional leadership fails to establish more effective regulatory standards and guidelines that we very possibly face a repeat of the problems that plagued the 2000 election cycle (Samples, Palmer, and Basham 2000). Consequently, the issue of regulating the federal campaign finance system in the United States tends to hinge upon an overloaded FEC—a regulatory agency that lacks adequate resources to accomplish its stated duties. Data in Table 3.2 provides general information concerning the relationship between FEC staff and a portion of the agency's overall workload, in this case, identified as FEC database entries.

In addition to these resource-related issues, a number of recent developments have emerged concerning the use of soft money and issue advocacy advertising in federal elections, particularly congressional elections. First, soft money—unregulated political funds—is now an essential part of campaign strategies in congressional elections. As soft money grows in importance, so do soft money contributors, because they give political parties the ability to shift millions of dollars into tight regional races. Second is issue advocacy advertising—advertisements broadcasting political messages without explicit advocacy for a candidate—increasingly used in competitive congressional elections by political interest groups and organizations. As political stakes increase and various campaign resources become scarcer, interest groups and political organizations focus their fight for control of Congress in strategic areas that might overwhelm a candidate's own campaign message. Thus, by using soft money and issue advocacy advertisements non-coordinated groups and organizations may erode candidate credibility and influence election outcomes, and by extension, the public policy process (Conlon 1987; Gais 1996).

Table 3.2.   FEC Database Entries and Staffing, 1986-2000

Year	Database Entries*	Staffing (FTE)
1986	526,000	229
1988	698,000	252
1990+	767,000	242
1992++	1,400,000	266
1994	1,364,000	293
1996	1,887,160	313
1998	1,652,904	313
2000	2,390,837	351

*Reflects cumulative total for each two-year cycle.
+Entry limit for individual contributions from $500 to $200 in 1989.
++Nonfederal account data first entered in 1991.
Source: *Federal Election Commission Annual Reports* (1975-2000).

For instance, the ability of non-party groups and organizations to mobilize grassroots activity in part decided the 1998 congressional elections. As an election cycle illustrates, although issue ads on television and radio are important, in low turnout midterm congressional elections, grassroots efforts (i.e., direct mail and telephone banks) become more important in deciding elections. Democrats and allied interests in 1998 were more effectively mobilized voters in the midterm election than did Republicans. Ultimately, political fortunes in federal elections may increasingly depend upon the use of these unregulated sources of political money (Magleby and Holt 1999).

These unregulated and undisclosed campaign activities, moreover, may lead to the further erosion of political efficacy in the United States by frustrating voters and candidates. For instance, multiple campaign messages create an atmosphere in which it is difficult to distinguish candidate communications from interest group or party organization communications. In addition, candidates face the unenviable possibility of being associated with any negative repercussions that may come about from the actions of outsiders, and thus, may cost the candidate the election (Magleby and Holt 1999). Thus, the use of soft money and advocacy spending in federal elections is changing the election process by allowing vast amounts of unreported money to determine, in part, the outcome of federal elections. Scholars such as Jacobson (1980), Drew (1983), Etzioni (1984), McFarland (1984), Sabato (1984, 1989),

Wright (1985), Hall and Wayman (1990), Sorauf (1992), Sabato and Simpson (1996) and government watchdog organizations such as Common Cause and Center for Responsive Politics monitor these developments. While more recent attempts to mitigate the problem of money in campaigns and elections continue, confusion still abounds. It is unlikely, however, that the use of money in federal elections will diminish in the near future.

Finally, it is important to note that in spite of its shortcomings, the very fact that there exists an FEC sets the United States election system apart from other industrialized democracies. Among the major industrialized democracies of the world, the United States is the only country to have a specific regulatory agency dedicated to the administration and enforcement of federal campaign finance law. While other countries, such as Canada, Germany, and Britain, have national committees and commissions to oversee parts of their national campaign finance system, only the United States has an independent regulatory agency. The FEC is the only federal-level regulatory agency with formal authority to enforce campaign finance law among the world leading industrialized democracies (Gunlicks 1993).

Conclusion

This chapter presented a historical overview of concerning efforts in the United States to regulate the campaign finance system in federal elections. Overall, the chapter documented the evolution of efforts to regulate the use of money to finance campaigns for federal office starting from the late 1800s to the present in the United States. This historical record indicated that over time the use of money in federal elections has grown to be not only more embedded into the election process, but increasingly complex as efforts to circumvent the law continues. To gain a better understanding of important political-administrative relationships concerning FEC administrative behavior, within this political context, it is necessary to conduct an empirical analysis. Before this analysis can occur, however, we need to develop and discuss an applied theoretical model that facilitates such analysis.

Chapter IV

A Theoretical Overview of the FEC

Following a review of the historical record of regulating campaign finances in the United States, it is necessary to outline the general environment and conditions in which the FEC exists. To accomplish this, the analysis uses organization theory to develop a clearer understanding of the relationship between political officials and FEC administrative behavior. This applied theoretical framework facilitates the analysis of how political officials use structural and management arrangements to influence the administrative behavior of the FEC concerning the administration and enforcement of campaign finance regulation.

This chapter examines the following toward developing a better theoretical and empirical understanding of this political-administrative relationship. First, there is a discussion of particular characteristics and attributes of organizations and organization theory. Second is a presentation of issues regarding organizational perspectives and decision-making. Third, there is an examination of an applied model of administrative arrangements illustrating political-administrative relationships and how administrative behavior depends on policy type and agency resources. This review is necessary to provide a clear understanding of where the FEC is organizational located in relation to institutional principals and highlight these hierarchical relationships.

The Nature of Organizations

Although the term organization theory suggests a singular account about organizations, the broader literature notes multiple organization theories based on various research agendas. Talcott Parsons (1956) provided the most concise explanation of these various research agendas by stating organization theory must be viewed as having three analytic perspectives: (1) organizational adaptation—*open system*; (2) organizational implementation—*closed system*; and (3) organizational integration—*social system*. The relevant literature indicates that while Parsons prefers an integration agenda, organizational research typically focuses on implementation with subsequent research on adaptation (Stern and Barley 1997). That said, because this project attempts to provide a comprehensive explanation of a political-administrative relationship, an integrated approach (i.e., adaptation and implementation) is used.

Regarding the study of the political-administrative dichotomy, a number of scholars recommend using organization theory as a model to structure the analysis (Katzmann 1980; White and Adams 1994; March 1997). Organization theory in its most general sense is valuable for facilitating a macro-examination of institutional sub-units focusing on the agency-level of analysis to identify what influences a unit's response to environmental factors. Studies using organization theory to model their analysis typically include the concepts of incrementalism, inertia, and adaptive learning (March and Simon 1958; Hall and Quinn 1983; March and Olsen 1984; Williamson 1990; Jenkins-Smith and Sabatier 1993). Organization theory structures the analysis of administrative agencies as two-dimensional with one dimension being contextual and the other being structural (Hatch 1997).

Since the FEC is an organization, it is necessary to begin with a discussion of how to define an organization. First, how are organizations unique from other social groups? Some scholars view organizations as formal collective units created by individuals to pursue some collective goal (Parson 1956; Scott 1975; Donaldson 1985; Desveaux 1995). This goal-oriented view of organizations implies that they are the product of a coordinated effort by like-minded individuals to achieve a certain goal that is not achievable through individual action (Pfeffer and Salancik 1978).

However, defining organizations in terms of goal-orientation is problematic for a number of reasons. First, there is the dilemma that many individuals within an organization either may not know or support the organization's goal. In addition, there is always the likelihood that even when an organization achieves its goal, the organization may develop new goals. This leads to the view that once created, organizations develop a new, more fundamental goal: maintaining and ensuring its continual survival (Tullock 1965; Downs 1967; Blau 1974; Kaufman 1976; Denhardt 1992; Hatch 1997; Pfeffer 1997). Therefore, rather than being strictly goal-oriented, organizations over time tend to focus more on establishing greater support to insure its survival (Pfeffer and Salancik 1978; Diamond 1993). Ultimately though, survival becomes if not the first and primary goal of organizations, it soon becomes at least an increasingly important and significant goal that influences organizational decision-making.

Second, organizations are distinguishable by the nature of their boundaries and their relationship with government. Organizational boundaries concern the issue that inclusion in an organization is something that an organization grants based upon an individual's desire to help it survive. In addition, the issue of organizational boundaries has to do with the reality that government formally recognizes an organization as a legitimate and autonomous entity. In this sense, public administrative agencies have a particular connection to the government because government confers legitimacy upon the organization and provides it with the necessary resources to survive (Barker 1990; Pfeffer 1997).

Third, to ensure its survival, organizations must induce other environmental actors to support it with essential resources (March and Simon 1958). According to this view, an organization survives only as long as it is able to induce voluntary resource contributions from suppliers necessary to maintain itself through remuneration. It is plausible then to assume that a government organization's survival is more problematic than survival of other non-government organizations because the acquisition of essential resources to maintain it can only come from specific government institutions. Because government organizations can only extract resources essential to its survival and legitimacy from specific government institutions, such as legislature, executive, and the judiciary, organization or administrative leadership must maintain amenable relations with members of Congress, the president, and members of the Supreme Court (Downs 1967; Pfeffer and Salancik 1978; Brumback 1991).

Therefore, we can say that government organizations are collective units with well-defined boundaries that attempt to accomplish set goals and continually seek to insure their existence while maintaining a special relationship with government resource providers. In the end though, all organizations tend to have at least one shared primary goal: survival (Pfeffer 1997). If this is the case then, it is necessary to examine how organizations make decisions that enhance their survival. Examining this type of information is important toward understanding the nexus between politics and administrative agencies if we are to better understand how the intrinsic ability of specific policies to direct certain political actions that eventually influences administrative behavior.

Organizational Perspectives and Decision-Making

As there is no universally agreed upon method for measuring administrative response to environmental elements, this research considers both contextual and structural factors (Allison 1971; Blau and Schoenherr 1971; Marshaw 1994; Donaldson 1996; Peters and Savoie 1996). To use an organization theory framework in the analysis of FEC administrative response to political officials requires consideration of relevant variables relevant (Waldo 1978; Donaldson 1996). A brief review of different organizational perspectives, however, is necessary before identifying specific political-administrative variables relevant to this specific analysis of the FEC.

Our understanding of organizations and their decision-making processes depends upon the particular perspective that we have of organizations. This is important because it is from a particular perspective of organizations that we develop and reinforce characteristics considered important to the operation and continued existence of specific organizations. Consideration of various organizational perspectives is also important regarding the appropriate theoretical and methodological approach to use when analyzing organizational action. It is necessary to determine which perspective is appropriate for analyzing FEC and political official relations regarding enforcement actions or "matter-under-review" (MUR).

The evolution of organizational perspectives is present in the literature. First, there is the classic perspective of organizations. This perspective characterizes organizations as machine-like, designed and constructed by management to achieve specific goals. According to this mechanistic organizational perspective, managers are engineers who design, build, and operate the organizational machine. The classic perspective focuses on organizational management and its influence on society. Typically, this perspective uses research methodologies such as observation, historical analysis, and personal reflection on experience to analyze organizations. Past studies using a mechanistic perspective indicate that using these types of methodologies to analyze an organization leads to the development of typologies, theoretical frameworks, and prescriptions for management (Hatch 1997). Classic studies by scholars who base their analysis according to this perspective of organizations include Adam Smith (1978), Karl Marx (1977), and Max Weber (1947).

Second, there is the modern perspective of organizations. This perspective characterizes organizations as a living system that performs the functions necessary to insure its survival by adapting its structure to fit its hostile environment. According to this organic perspective of organizations, managers are an interdependent part of an adaptive organizational environment. The modern perspective of organizations focuses on the analysis of organizations by using objective measures. Past studies using the organic perspective, contend that using this type of methodology to analyze organizations leads to the development of descriptive and standardized measures of performance. In addition, this research indicates that using objective methodologies to analyze organizations leads to the development of comparative studies, statistical analysis, and descriptive findings (Hatch 1997). Scholars who use this modern perspective of organizations in their analysis include Talcott Parsons (1956), Herbert Simon (1957), and James March (1997). However, from either the mechanistic or the organic view of organizations, one can develop fundamental organizational characteristics that are important to the analysis and understanding of an organization's decision-making process.

Organizational decision-making refers to the hierarchical processes by which unit leadership determines an organization's actions (Bell 1985; Leibenstein 1987; Light 1995). Scholars of seminal studies examining the importance of organizational decision-making include James March (1958, 1963), Herbert Simon (1958), and Richard Cyert (1963). These scholars emphasize the political aspects of the organizational decision-making process and establish a division between economic and political explanations of organizational decision-making. Economists traditionally explain organizational decision-making based on the assumption of rationality. Simon, March, and Cyert, however questions this assumption of rationality. Instead, these scholars offer observational evidence that organizational decision-making processes can only be termed rational under restrictive conditions. Contrary to economic assumptions of rationality in the decision-making process as originating from the economic literature, Simon, March, and Cyert contend that politics greatly influences organizational decision-making.

Thus, competing explanations of the organizational decision-making process follow from a particular perspective of the organization. According to the mechanistic view of organizations used by classical scholars, the decision-making process in organizations is primarily rational and economical. In comparison, the organic view of organizations contends not only that the decision-making process in organization is less rational than the mechanistic view could have one believe, but also that the organizational decision-making process is primarily political. Note that the comparison of these two views of organizations does not advocate that one view is better than the other but only that a particular view may provide more meaningful research results depending upon the analysis. Because of these differing explanations of the organizational decision-making process, an analysis of related and important theoretical assumptions underpinning both explanations is necessary.

Critical Theoretical Assumptions

Assumptions about the nature of the decision-making process in the political science literature are characteristic of the economic-based rational choice approach (Von Neumann and Morgenstern 1944; Downs 1957; Arrow 1974; North 1990; Ostrom 1991; McLean 1991; Heap, Hollis, Lyons, Sugden, and Weale 1992; Morrow 1994). The traditional rational choice approach assumes self-interested individuals act rationally in pursuit of their own health, and therefore, determine organizational decisions. This self-interest, however, does not imply that individuals do not care for others. Rather, self-interest simply means that individuals put their own interests ahead of others when these interests conflict. The implication of this assumption of self-interested rationality is that we cannot rely solely on good nature to ensure that individuals act in the interests of others. This assumes that because the rational decision-making process determines organizational action, it is necessary to develop incentives that align individual interests with organizational objectives (Pfeffer 1997).

Simon, however, questions the assumptions of the rational decision-making process on two points. First, Simon contends that in reality, decision-makers often possess incomplete and imperfect information about alternatives and consequences. Second, this assumption of strict rationality ignores the internal politics of organizations concerning preference ordering and rules. Therefore, Simon proposes that attempts by decision-makers in organizations to make purely rational decisions are limited due to (a) imperfect and incomplete information, (b) problem complexity, (c) human information processing capacity, (d) time constraints, and (e) conflicting preferences. Simon contends due to bounded rationality, decision-makers' rationale for organizational decisions are limited.

Two implications of bounded rationality are important concerning the analysis organizations. First, because decision-makers have too little information to meet the demands of the rational decision-making process, difficulties associated with organizational change and environmental complexity produces uncertainty among decision-makers. More precisely, due to the cost of acquiring more information is so great decision-makers either foregoes these costs or creates shortcuts to keep costs at a minimum. Second, because of conflicting goals and preferences among decision-makers, the decision-making process may become ambiguous. Ultimately, because bounded rationality acknowledges the presence of uncertainty and ambiguity in the decision-making process, it provides a more realistic framework for understanding the decision-making process in a government organization such as the FEC. Nonetheless, it is necessary to examine the causes for the presence of uncertainty. Even if decision-makers can agree on what their collective goals and preferences should be, disagreement may continue regarding which among multiple alternatives they should select. Regardless of cost or conflicts, successful decision-makers understand that for any decision to produce the desired outcome, it is imperative to consider the organization's environment.

The Organizational Environment of the FEC

Organization theory conceptualizes the environment of an organization as the surrounding area that interacts with the organization (Mainzer 1973). This environment influences the organization's behavior by imposing constraints and demands on the organization. For its part, the organization learns to adapt to these multiple demands in order to survive (Eavery and Miller 1984; Mazmanian and Sabatier 1989; Lebovic 1995). It is in this hostile environment that the organization must not only adapt to multiple demands, but also depend upon other environmental elements within the environment to provide it with necessary resources to sustain it (Pfeffer and Salancik 1978). Therefore, due to the contentious nature of an organization's relationship with its environment, it becomes necessary to specify exactly what environmental elements may influence its behavior. For the purpose of this research, it is helpful to consider and discuss what environmental elements may influence the agency's administrative behavior, specifically, FEC initiation of MURs over time.

To begin, it is necessary to define the organizational environment of the FEC. First, there is the intra-organizational network of the FEC. The intra-organizational network refers the environmental area around the FEC where elements that are in continuous interact with the agency (i.e., legislature, executive, and judiciary). On the one hand, political institutions at are continuously interacting with the FEC supply the agency with essential operational resources. On the other hand, the FEC also provides services to these other intra-organizational elements—regulatory and administrative services—necessary to their health (Bates and Bianco 1990). This intra-organizational network is therefore a complex web of relationships in which the FEC and political officials are embedded and mutually dependent (Bendor and Mookherjee 1987).

Second, there is the general environment of the FEC. The general environment of the FEC includes the intra-organizational network and more remote sectors that tend to have a broader influence on the organization. These broader environmental sectors have an effect throughout the environment and upon one another. Therefore, an overview of the agency's general environment is necessary to appreciate the large-scale links between the agency, institutional elements, and broader socioeconomic sectors. Although this research does not analyze these factors extensively, nonetheless, it is important to note their presence.

This overview of the general environment of the FEC requires dividing this environment into various sectors. The general environment of the FEC includes social, cultural, legal, political, economic, technological, and physical sectors. The social sector is associated with class structure, demographics, mobility patterns, lifestyles, and traditional social institutions, including educational systems, religious practices, trades, and professions. The cultural sector is associated with issues such as history, traditions, expectations for behavior, and the values of the society. The legal sector is associated with the constitution, federal law and legal practice in the United States. The political sector is associated with the distribution and concentration of power and the nature of the American political system. The economic sector is associated with labor, financial, and commercial markets. The technological sector is associated with knowledge and information in the form of scientific developments that the FEC acquires and uses to regulate the FECA. The physical sector is associated with nature and natural resources (Hatch 1997). The ability of these environmental factors, individually and collectively, to influence an organization's actions is significant.

To understand the crosscutting influences of the different contingent environmental elements requires paying special attention to the theoretical framework used in this analysis. Specifically, note that this analysis of the various contingency factors is in essence an analysis of the different aspects of a single, diverse, complex, and integrated environment. The FEC, as such, is not separate from its environment, but is in fact a fundamental element of this environment. The FEC exists within an intra-organizational network that, in turn, exists within a broader, general environment with multiple sectors. The critical point is that the FEC is not simply a member of this environment, but an integral part of its environment. As such, to view the agency's behavior outside the context of its environment would lead to results that are not consistent with reality.

Related to organization-environment relationship is the decision-making process within the FEC. In particular is the inability of organizational leadership to agree on a single set of goals. This situation is the result of multiple goals, conflicting views, resource competition, interdependence, and inherent contradictions due to the complex and diverse contingencies radiating from the environment. Thus, individuals within the FEC occupying the most powerful decision-making positions have to decide how the organization interprets and implements policy. Because FEC decision-makers are aware of the tendency not to fully agree on administrative and enforcement matters and goals, they may attempt to manage the decision-making process by engaging in politics. Politics may be defined in this case briefly as a process whereby a group of people, whose opinions or interests are initially divergent, reach collective decisions which are generally regarded as binding on the group, and enforced as common policy (Miller 1991).

In situations that fit the conditions of a coalition model of decision-making, nonetheless, ambiguity is far more problematic than uncertainty within an organization. Under these conditions, FEC decision-makers do not focus primarily on a search for problem-solving information, but rather emphasize interest-accommodating alternatives. Although the development of a coalition implies a breakdown of the traditional organization decision-making process, this type of accommodation is a reasonable basis for facilitating organizational decision-making in the context of institutional relationships. Over time, however, power differentials between institutional-organization units develop due to ability of an institution to provide scarce, non-replaceable goods to an organization. The balance of power between the two tilts in the favor of the institution because institutional officials can manipulate non-replaceable agency resources (i.e., budget, legislation, appointments, judicial actions) (Crozier 1964; Hatch 1997). An institution's ability to determine organizational uncertainty, therefore, results in a power differential between the agent and principal that compounds the problem of organization ambiguity.

Additional research shows that it is not only uncertainty that produces various power differentials, but also the organization's ability to cope with uncertainty by using preventive, forecasting, and absorption tactics (Hatch 1997). However, coping with uncertainty does not negate the fact that hierarchical dominant institutions control arrangements that are critical to the existence of the subordinate organization for which there are no substitutes (Hickson, Hinings, Lee, Schneck, and

Pennings 1971). Specifically regarding the FEC, this dependence on these non-replaceable resources determines the power differential between the agency and political officials in legislative, executive, and judicial institutions. This perspective provides a meaningful way to look at the agency's relationship with other elements within its environment.

Administrative Arrangement Model

An administrative arrangement model helps to explain the linkage between environmental factors such as institutional officials and organizational action via political processes. According to this model, environmental contingencies, such as scarcity of essential resources, and hierarchically determined administrative arrangements create organizational uncertainties that translate into power differentials. The environmental contingencies therefore tend to influence the behavior of the organization's decision-makers. Accordingly, organization decision-makers respond to these contingencies by developing measures that (1) ensure the organization's survival and (2) increase the probability of attaining planned unit outcomes.

There are several basic premises of the administrative arrangement model. First, the fundamental unit for understanding this environmental relationship is the organization. Second, the organization is constrained by a network of interdependencies with other elements. Third, this network of interdependencies, coupled with organizational ambiguity and institutional uncertainty, leads to a situation in which the organization's survival becomes questionable. Fourth, the organization develops measures to manage external interdependencies and uncertainty that may themselves produce new constraints and interdependencies. Fifth, these new constraints and dependencies produce intra-organizational power, which in turn may lead to a particular decision-making process that determines administrative behavior. An organization, in the end, must continuously attempt to deal with these environmental demands in such a manner as to ensure its survival (Pfeffer 1982; West 1995; see Webb and Weick 1979).

At a fundamental level then, FEC vulnerability to its environment is due to its structure and management arrangements. Political officials in this environment—the president, Congress, and the Supreme Court—control these arrangements. Reliance on these arrangements gives political officials in the agency's environment power over organization decision-makers, and thus, influences the agency's administrative behavior (Buchanan, Tollison, and Tullock 1980; Tullock 1989). The complexity of the administrative arrangement position of the FEC is primarily due to its need to develop cooperative relationships with political officials and related interests that exist in the agency's intra-organizational network (Teske 1991). Analysis of FEC administrative behavior using an administrative arrangement model begins by identifying the environment (Kaufman 1973, 1981). Note that this political-administrative model only accounts for political influence on administrative behavior.

The model focuses on environmental actors that influence FEC administrative behavior, thereby affecting the agency's initiation of enforcement actions. According to this framework then, FEC initiation of a MUR is, in part, is a function of how political officials determine agency arrangements and thus influence FEC decision-makers to adapt to these external contingencies. The expectation is that the FEC responses to political determination of administrative arrangements by adapting its behavior to fit its environment (Terry 1990, 1995; Moe and Wilson 1994; Donaldson 1996).

Conclusion

This chapter described how using organization theory assists in the analysis of relationships between political officials and FEC organizational behavior over time. The use of the administrative arrangement approach explains environment links to organizational behavior via political processes. This approach contends that environmental constraints and contingencies provoke organizational uncertainties that produce opportunities for agency decision-makers to cope with by adapting administrative behaviors that ensures its survival in a hostile environment. Using the applied theoretical model helps to orient the research and assists in developing testable hypotheses that allow for an empirical evaluation of FEC administrative behavior in relation institutional officials in a political context over time. Before this can begin, however, an overview of the FEC is necessary to acknowledge institutional constraints on agency decision-makers.

Chapter V

The Federal Election Commission: An Overview

This chapter provides an overview of how the FEC administers and enforces federal campaign finance law. To begin, there is a summary of the establishment and structure of the FEC that provides a concise view of the agency, focusing on decision-makers and leadership positions. Following is an examination of the administrative and enforcement processes used by the FEC for maintaining the federal electoral process. The chapter concludes with analysis and commentary about agency enforcement procedures that provide some insight into addressing the primary normative concern of this analysis. Analyzing administrative arrangements with regard to policy outputs and outcomes requires this organizational overview.

An Overview of the FEC

Because legislation and statutes are not self-executing, Congress designates the FEC to administer and enforce campaign finance law. The establishment of the FEC is a significant development toward the continuing effort of safeguarding and enhancing democratic elections and the campaign system in the United States. The four primary duties of the FEC are (a) disclosure of campaign finance information; (b) administration of the presidential election public funds; (c) clearinghouse for election related material; and (d) enforcement of federal campaign finance laws (*Federal Election Commission: Twenty Year Report*, April 1995). This section provides a general overview of the FEC and the agency's efforts to enforce the law. First, a review of the establishment of the FEC is necessary.

Establishment of the FEC

Although Congress established strict campaign finance provisions in 1971 with the FECA (P.L. 92-225) and the Revenue Act (P.L 92-178), it failed to address a primary shortcoming of these and past efforts to regulate elections. Like previous legislation, the 1971 Acts did not provide a single, independent regulatory agency to monitor and enforce campaign finance law. Instead of a single independent regulatory agency, the Clerk of the House, the Secretary of the Senate and the General Accounting Office (GAO) monitored campaign material for compliance with the law. In addition, the Department of Justice was responsible for enforcing and prosecuting violations of the campaign finance law referred by Congressional and GAO officials. However, following reports of corruption in the 1972 presidential elections and the Department of Justice failure to prosecute violators, campaign finance reform moved to the forefront of government's policy agenda (*Comptroller General of the United States*, 1975).

The 1974 amendments to the FECA (P.L. 93-443) create the FEC for the purpose of administrating and enforcing federal campaign finance law as outlined in the FECA. Because of the 1974 FECA Amendments, the FEC now serves as the independent regulatory agency that has administration responsibilities previously divided among congressional officers and the General Accounting Office. In addition, the FEC assumed some of the enforcement responsibilities previously held solely by the Department of Justice. Thus, the FEC has jurisdiction over campaign finance related civil enforcement matters, authority to write campaign finance regulation, and responsibility for monitoring and enforcing compliance with the FECA. Further, the 1974 FECA Amendments transferred from the GAO to the FEC the function of serving as the national clearinghouse for information on federal election administration. Thus, the FEC has become the primary organization responsible for the administration and enforcement of federal campaign finance law.

Three other federal agencies, however, share some of the regulatory responsibilities with the FEC concerning campaign finance enforcement and administration. First, the Department of Justice may receive referrals from the FEC to prosecute criminal violations of the FECA and refer matters to the agency when appropriate. Second, the Department of the Treasury disburses public funds to presidential candidates certified by the FEC as meeting statutory eligibility requirements. Also, the Internal Revenue Service (IRS) reviews FEC regulation for consistency with U.S. tax codes, interprets which political activities result in taxable income, and determines whether an organization's political activity is consistent with its claimed status under tax law. Third, the FCC monitors broadcaster compliance with federal guidelines in providing federal candidates reasonable access to purchase broadcast time at the lowest rates possible. Therefore, while the FEC takes the lead in the administration and enforcement of campaign finance law, it operates in unison with other federal agencies and offices.

A review of the hierarchical structure of the FEC is necessary to understand how it administrates and enforces campaign finance law. Because organizations such as the FEC are too complex to operate through a simple structure, they adopt a functional structure as a means of coping with the increasing demands of differentiation. The functional structure of the FEC is advantageous because it groups activities according to similar work activities, tasks, and goals. This functional structure is also efficient because it limits duplication of effort and tends to maximize economies of scale from specialization. Figure 5.1 illustrates the functional structure of the FEC. As of FY2000, the FEC established the Office of Administrative Review and the Office of Alternative Dispute Resolution.

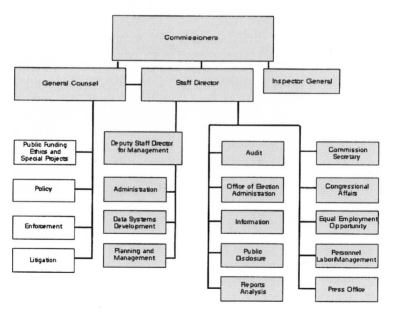

Figure 5.1.   FEC Organization Chart.
Source: *Federal Election Commission: Twenty-Year Report, April 1995.*

First, there is the FEC Commission. The Commission has six voting members who serve staggered six-year terms. Appointment of commissioners is by the President with the advice and consent of the Senate. In addition, according to the FECA, no more then three Commissioners may belong to the same political party. The Commissioners elect two members each year to act as Chairman and Vice Chairman. Commissioners generally meet twice a week, once in closed session to discuss confidential matters and once in an open session to discuss public matters. At these meetings, Commissioners develop policy and vote on significant legal and administrative issues. Commissioners serve full-time and are responsible for administering and enforcing the FECA. In general, individuals appointed to serve on the Commission usually have professional backgrounds in party politics, law, or academia.

Second, there is the Office of Inspector General. The Office of Inspector General focuses its efforts on promoting efficient and effective administrative management and identifying organizational problems. As part of its duties, the Office of Inspector General has the dual reporting responsibility of keeping agency decision-makers and Congress informed concerning FEC operations, administration, and problems. The Office of Inspector General produces Semiannual Reports and Audit Reports that provides FEC management and Congress with up-to-date information concerning the agency's activities. Based upon the Office of Inspector General findings and recommendations found in the reports, administrative officials in the FEC may implement new policy and procedural changes that enhance the organization's overall effectiveness and efficiency. It is important to note that because the Office of Inspector General does not perform a program operating function, the office does not have an adversary relationship with agency administrative officials or Congress. Perhaps because of its unique administrative position, it can develop cooperative relationships with agency and political officials that aim to improve the agency's regulatory performance.

Third, there is the Staff Director's Office. The Staff Director's Office oversees the appointment of personnel to particular positions with the approval of the Commission. The Staff Director, who is selected and serves at the pleasure of the Commissioners, oversees the Commission's public disclosure activities, promotional efforts, reviews and prepares reports for the Commissioners' consideration, the agency's audit program, and general administration of the agency. The Deputy Staff Director is responsible for assisting the Staff Director in the areas of budget, administration, and computer systems supervision. Overall, the Staff Director's Office is responsible for the day-to-day operations of the FEC and for the implementation of many agency long-term administrative plans.

Fourth, there is the Office of General Counsel of the FEC. The Office of General Counsel, headed by the General Counsel, is responsible for directing the agency's enforcement activities. General Counsel represents and advises the Commission in any legal actions brought before it, and serves as Designated Agency Ethics Official. The Office also handles all civil litigation, including Title 26 cases concerning presidential elections that come before the Supreme Court. The office drafts Advisory Opinions and regulation that interpret federal campaign finance laws for the Commission's consideration.

The Office of General Counsel has four separate divisions. The Public Financing, Ethics, and Special Projects Division that is responsible for the public funding system, review of audit reports, and special projects. The Policy Division is responsible for providing Advisory Opinions, regulatory review, process reconsideration requests, and review of the FECA. The Litigation Division that is responsible for civil enforcement activities for the FEC, and thus, engages in offensive and defensive litigation processes. The Enforcement Division that has the primary responsible for implementing the agency's overall enforcement administration that includes efforts at conciliation and determination of specific punishments when authorized by the Commissioners. Due to the functional-structural design of this and all units of the FEC, agency leadership maintains hierarchical power and control over agency activities.

FEC Administration and Enforcement of the Law

According to the FECA, the FEC is responsible for developing and administrating a conciliatory enforcement style concerning its regulation of the federal campaign finance system to avoid infringing upon electoral rights and freedoms. FEC actions to encourage voluntary compliance begin early in an election cycle. First, political committees contact the FEC initially by way of the agency's toll-free information line. As questions about filing the proper paperwork for federal campaigns increase during the election cycle, political committee staff may use various FEC services to ensure they comply with the law. During the early stages of an election cycle, the Information Office is usually the first FEC unit to interact with political committees.

The Information Office of the FEC explains requirements of federal campaign law to political campaign committees, candidates, and other interested groups. In addition, the Information Office sends reminder notices along with the necessary reporting forms to registered campaign committees shortly before reports are due and provides free publications on request. Finally, the Audit Division of the FEC assists presidential committees in complying with the special rules for publicly funded campaigns and encourages campaign committee members to attend FEC instructional workshops and conferences.

When a committee files a report with the FEC, the agency's Public Records Office ensures that a copy is available for public inspection within 48 hours of receipt. When political committees submit registration documents the Data Systems and Development Division of the FEC assigns each an identification number and enters registration information into the FEC database. Microfilm and paper copies of the registration become part of the public record, as the political committees are automatically on the agency's mailing list for official notices and correspondence.

A fundamental responsibility of the FEC is to provide public access to the campaign finance reports the agency maintains. In the Public Records Office, the public can review microfilms, paper copies, and the agency's computer database for committee report information. On-line computer access to political committees' financial data is also available to the public at state offices using the agency's State Access Program and to individual subscribers linked on-line to the Direct Access Program. The Direct Access Program provides access to raw financial data organized by categorical indexes. The FEC also provides a variety of other resources that include Advisory Opinions, closed enforcement and litigation files, audit reports, and Commission meetings minutes. Finally, media organizations may review committee reports using any of the methods described above and receive assistance from the Press Office of the FEC. Press Office Staff answer reporters' questions issue press releases summarizing campaign finance data and significant FEC actions, and respond to requests under the Freedom of Information Act. However, despite FEC efforts to encourage voluntary compliance through its many outreach programs, none of its efforts would be successful without meaningful, effective and credible enforcement.

Enforcement of Campaign Finance Laws

As extensive as FEC efforts are at encouraging voluntary compliance with federal campaign finance laws, these efforts would nonetheless, be irrelevant without the threat of punishment. Following *Buckley v. Valeo* (1976), the House Administration Committee changed FEC

regulatory procedures and processes to establish a voluntary enforcement model similar to that of the Equal Employment Opportunity
Commission (Gormley 1998). The FEC uses general staff lawyers and
auditors that conduct much of their investigation from Washington, DC
via long-distance telephone calls and written questions cleared in advance by agency superiors (Jackson 1990).

   The first stage of the enforcement process is the receipt and consideration of a complaint. Upon initiation of a regulatory investigation,
the FEC enforcement model requires that the agency decide whether it
has "cause-to-believe" that the respondent violated the law. Possible
violations that may come under consideration are either internally generated cases or externally generated cases. Internally generated cases
come from either Director 6, the Reports Analysis Division, *sua
sponte*, or from other government agencies. The majority of internally
generated investigations are the result of the agency's own monitoring
system. The Reports Analysis Division reviews each committee report
in order to ensure the accuracy of the information on the public record
and to monitor for compliance with the law. If information in a report
appears to be incomplete or inaccurate, the Reports Analysis Division
sends the committee a "request-for-additional-information." Having
received this "request-for-additional-information," the committee may
avoid an audit or judicial action by responding promptly to the request.
Usually, those receiving a "request-for-additional-information" respond
by returning an amended form with the required information. Further,
the FEC can also conduct an official audit of a political committee "for
cause" when a review of a committee's report indicates a purposeful
violation of the campaign finance law. Once an internal source determines that there is a possible violation of campaign finance law, the
case goes to the Office of General Counsel's Enforcement Division. It
is at this point that the case receives a pre-MUR number. Internally
generated cases receive a formal MUR number once the Commission
has found a "reason-to-believe" during the second stage of the enforcement process.

   Externally generated cases come from any source outside the FEC
or the government. Any person may file a complaint with the FEC if
they believe a violation of campaign finance law has occurred or is
about to occur. The complaint must be in writing and submitted to the
FEC along with three copies. The complaint must also provide the full
name and address of the person filing the complaint along with a
signed, sworn to, and notarized statement. To consider a complaint
complete and proper, it must specifically indicate what the violation is
under FEC jurisdiction and identify each party that alleged to have

committed the violation with supporting documentation. Further, the complaint must differentiate between statements according to the complainant's personal knowledge and statements according to the belief that identify the source of the information. If the complaint does not meet the criteria for investigation, the Office of General Counsel will reject the compliant and notify the complainant that they may re-submit the matter.

Following the Office of General Counsel's Enforcement Division and Special Assistant review of an alleged violation, it is necessary to determine if (a) the complaint is proper and (b) the complaint meets threshold criteria for further investigation. If the case meets these criteria then it is forwarded to the Office of General Counsel's Enforcement Division where assigned a MUR number. However, if the Office of General Counsel finds that the (a) complaint is not proper or (b) that the complaint does not meet threshold criteria for further investigation, the complainant and respondent are notified of the rejection. If the Office of General Counsel determines that the filing of the case is proper and meets criteria for further investigation, the Enforcement Division places the case on the Central Enforcement Docket. The case at this point is then given to the Office of General Counsel's Assistant General Counsel, Associate General Counsel, and the General Counsel for additional consideration concerning if further investigation is necessary. If the Office of General Counsel determines that no further investigation is necessary, then the case and MUR number are closed. The Office of General Counsel then notifies the complainant and respondent why no further investigation is necessary and closes the case. However, if the Office of General Counsel concludes that further investigation is necessary, the General Counsel will prepare a case report for the MUR that then goes to the six FEC Commissioners for consideration.

The second stage of the enforcement process is the "reason-to-believe" stage. Following the Office of General Counsel's review, a case report goes to FEC Commissioners with a recommendation that additional investigation concerning a particular case is necessary. If the Commission votes to disagree with the Office of General Counsel's recommendation that further investigation is necessary, then a discussion with the General Counsel concerning the case conducted. However, if the Commission concurs with the Office of General Counsel's recommendation that further investigation is necessary, then the Commission must determine if there is "reason-to-believe" that a violation occurred, or that there is "no-reason-to-believe" that a violation has occurred. At this point, the Commission can take one of three possible actions: (1) conclude that there is "no-reason-to-believe" and close the case; (2) conclude that there is "reason-to-believe," but "take-no-further-action" and close the case; or (3) find that there is "reason-to-believe" and continue the investigation. If the Commission finds "reason-to-believe," then the FEC sends a letter notifying the respondent of this finding. The letter requests a written reply to allegations of wrong-doing and may include supplemental questions. In addition, the FEC may issue orders requiring sworn written answers and subpoenas that call for an individual to testify or to produce specific documents. If necessary, the FEC may ask a federal district court to enforce these orders and subpoenas. The investigation may also include less formal procedures, such as interviews involving parties other than the respondent who may have important information concerning the complaint.

The third stage of the enforcement process is the "probable-cause" stage. After completing its investigation, the Office of General Counsel prepares a brief that explains factual and legal issues of the case and recommends whether the Commission should find there is "probable-cause-to-believe," a violation has occurred or is about to occur. The respondent receives a copy of the brief and has 15 days to file a reply brief explaining the respondent's position. Before the Commission mails the respondent the Office of General Counsel's brief containing "probable-cause-to-believe" recommendations, the respondent may request, in writing, that the matter be resolved through conciliation negotiations. Pre-probable cause discussions may lead to a conciliation agreement between the respondent and the Commission, thereby re-solving the matter. If the matter is resolved at this point, the MUR case is closed.

If the conciliation agreement process cannot resolve the matter, however, the Commission sends the respondent the brief. The respondent has 15 days to submit a reply brief. After reviewing briefs from the Office of General Counsel and the respondent, the Commissioners vote on whether there is "probable-cause-to-believe." If the Commissioners decide there is "no-probable-cause-to-believe" the MUR case is closed and the parties notified. If the Commission—by four affirmative votes—determines that there is "probable-cause-to-believe" that a violation of the law has occurred, the MUR case remains open and the Office of General Counsel attempts to correct or prevent the violation through informal conciliation methods. If the Office of General Counsel and the respondent negotiate a conciliation agreement at this point, the written agreement becomes effective following four affirmative votes by the Commissioners and a signed agreement between the respondent and Office of General Counsel. The agreement usually includes a description of the facts and the law, admissions of the violations by the respondent, any remedial actions the respondent must take, and a provision for the payment of a civil penalty by the respondent. The Office of General Counsel sends a copy of the signed agreement to the respondent and complainant when the MUR case is closed.

The fourth and final stage of the enforcement process is conciliation. The agency must attempt to resolve all enforcement matters through conciliation. The FEC routinely proposes conciliation agreements with the stipulation that the accused admits to the violation that is consistent with the agency's finding of "reason-to-believe" that there is a violation of the law. If conciliation fails, however, the FEC, rather than the Department of Justice, may take a respondent to court. Likewise, when there are challenges concerning FEC legal actions, the regulatory agency conducts its own legal defensive using agency lawyers. Concerning cases appealed to the Supreme Court, however, the FEC cannot unilaterally bring cases before it, except those involving the Presidential Public Funding program. Instead, the FEC must ask the Department of Justice either to represent the agency or to grant approval for the FEC to represent itself before the Court. Figure 5.2 outlines the four-stage administrative enforcement process of the FEC. A review of the agency's enforcement process illustrates a long, complex, and exhaustive practice characterized by numerous internal checkpoints during which agency decision-makers can interrupt the enforcement investigation process. The fragility of the agency's enforcement process leads to the conventional wisdom that enforcement efforts tend to be ineffective.

To protect the interests of those involved in a complaint, the FECA requires that any Commission action concerning an enforcement investigation remain confidential until the case is resolved. This provision of confidentiality however does not prevent a complainant or respondent from disclosing the substance of the enforcement investigation to other interests or the media. Nevertheless, information about an official FEC notification of findings or about an enforcement investigation is confidential unless the respondent waives the right to confidentiality in writing. A MUR case is available to the public in the Press Office and the Office of Public Records within 30-days after the case is closed and all relevant parties notified.

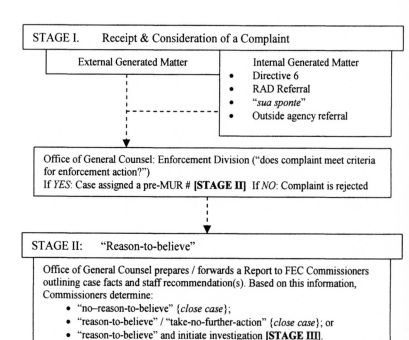

STAGE I.   Receipt & Consideration of a Complaint

External Generated Matter	Internal Generated Matter
	• Directive 6
	• RAD Referral
	• *"sua sponte"*
	• Outside agency referral

Office of General Counsel: Enforcement Division ("does complaint meet criteria for enforcement action?")
If *YES*: Case assigned a pre-MUR # **[STAGE II]** If *NO*: Complaint is rejected

STAGE II: "Reason-to-believe"

Office of General Counsel prepares / forwards a Report to FEC Commissioners outlining case facts and staff recommendation(s). Based on this information, Commissioners determine:
• "no–reason-to-believe" {*close case*};
• "reason-to-believe" / "take-no-further-action" {*close case*}; or
• "reason-to-believe" and initiate investigation **[STAGE III]**.

STAGE III: "Probable-cause"

Office of General Counsel completes its investigation and forwards a brief explaining factual / legal issues to Commissioners that recommends whether the Commission should find there is "probable-cause-to-believe" a violation has occurred. Based on this information, Commissioners determine:
• "no–probable-cause" and notify involved parties {*close case*};
• "probable-cause" and negotiate a conciliation agreement {*close case*}; or
• "probable-cause" and attempt conciliation agreement **[STAGE IV]**.

STATE IV: "Conciliation"

The FEC must attempt to resolve all enforcement matters through conciliation.
• Conciliation agreements / accused admitting to violation {*close case*};
• If 'conciliation" fails, FEC may take the accused to court {*close case*}; or
• If case is appealed to the Supreme Court, the FEC must ask the Department of Justice to either (a) represent the agency or (b) to grant approval for the FEC to represent itself.

Figure 5.2.   Overview of FEC Enforcement Process.

A review of the FEC enforcement process provides a number of interesting findings. First, there are a number of points during the process at which non-elected staff and appointees may slowdown or end an investigation. Second, this process that involves procedures and language that seem to increase rather than reduce ambiguity, may in fact contribute toward increasing confusion and distrust regarding investigation of possible violations of the FECA. Third, because Congress mandates that the FEC focus on conciliatory regulatory enforcement cases are rarely resolved in a timely manner. While the presentation of the enforcement process appears simple, its true complexity eludes easy representation. Following are short case studies that provide examples illustrating each stage of the FEC enforcement process.

FEC Enforcement Stages Case Studies
Stage One Example: Receipt & Consideration of a Complaint

U.S. Court of Appeals for the District of Columbia Circuit (94-5216), D.Ct. No. 91-2428, on November 3, 1995 remands this case to the district court with instructions to dismiss for lack of jurisdiction. Absalom Jordan brought this case before the courts seeking judicial review of the FEC decision to dismiss an administrative complaint he had filed. When Mr. Jordan receives the FEC letter of the dismissal, he has 53 days left on the 60-day limit in which to file suit. He did not file suit until 63 days after the FEC voted to dismiss his complaint. The Court rules in favor of the FEC, upholding its decision to dismiss the complaint. Under 2 U.S.C. §437g(a)(8)(B), a petition to review an FEC decision to dismiss an administrative complaint must be filed within 60 days after the date of dismissal. According to the Court, the 60-day period began when the Commission voted to dismiss the complaint, and not on the date of the FEC letter informing Mr. Jordan of the dismissal. Thus, the Appeals Court lacks jurisdiction to review this case. On January 23, 1996, the District Court carries out the Court's instructions to dismiss this case.

While this case highlights initiation of enforcement, it also notes that an action of this sort is not administratively classified as an administrative enforcement action. Unfortunately, the FEC does not maintain data of cases reviewed but not assigned a MUR number. If this type of information were available, an analysis of the data might not only additional information concerning agency efficiency when processing reports of possible FECA violations, but also information concerning the nature of reported violations. For instance, it would be valuable to analysis the data and see if certain groups, organizations, or interests routinely file inconsequential violation reports with the FEC for the purpose of "overloading" the agency's administrative enforcement apparatus.

Stage Two Example: "Reason to Believe"

In MUR 4320, D.H. Blair & Co. Inc., a New York City brokerage firm, faced charges that some of its employees used political committee contributor lists obtained from the FEC for commercial purposes. The list facilitated the making of "cold calls" to potential clients, in violation of the "sale and use restriction" of federal law (2 U.S.C. &438(a)(4)). This particular MUR case is an example of an internally generated MUR due to a referral from the Public Records Office of the FEC. Agency staffers working in the Public Records Office questioned an individual's request and review of this public information. Beginning in late 1994, an employee in the Public Records Office noticed an unusual pattern of requests for lists of individual contributors traceable to D.H. Blair. The Public Records Office referred the matter to the FEC Office of General Counsel. The result of this referral was a review of preliminary information and the subsequent assignment of a pre-MUR number. Based on preliminary information, the Commission found "reason-to-believe" that D.H. Blair knowingly and willfully violated the law. When notified of the Commission's "reason-to-believe" finding, D.H. Blair denied knowingly and willfully violated the law. However, before the Commission's finding "probable-cause-to-believe" the law had been violated, Blair agreed to enter into a conciliation agreement with the Commission and pay a civil penalty. This example shows that when initiated, cases that the General Counsel's Office determines demonstrates a significant violation of the FECA, once assigned a MUR enforcement case number, can motivate all parties to seek conciliation to remedy the alleged violation.

Stage Three Example: "Probable Cause"

In MUR 4322 and 4650, the Commission found that Enid Greene, of Enid Greene 1994 and 1996 campaign committees, and other persons violated campaign finance law in several ways related to the her 1994 and 1996 Congressional campaigns. These violations included (a) commingling campaign funds with personal funds, (b) making and accepting contributions in the names of another, (c) filing inaccurate reports, and (d) making and accepting excessive contributions beyond lawful limits. Initiation of this enforcement investigation and subsequent MUR 4322 is the result of an external report submitted to the FEC from Michael H. Chanin, Esq., Counsel for Enid 1994 and Enid

1996. Further, the Reports Analysis Division of the FEC initiated MUR 4650 according to information originally generated by MUR4322. With regard to each violation of the FECA, the FEC Commissioners found that the evidence provided adequate support for a finding of "reason-to-believe." This "reason-to-believe" allowed the Office of General Council to conduct additional and more intensive investigations into this matter. Later because the Commission found "probable-cause" that the stated violations had occurred, conciliation agreements were established with Enid Green, Forest Greene, and the two campaign committees agreeing to pay a $100,000 joint civil penalty. Because of Joseph Waldholtz's incarceration and personal finance problems, due to his criminal conviction on 27 counts of bank fraud, his conciliation agreement did not include civil penalty. This case shows that enforcement initiation and a "reason-to-believe" finding that a violation did occur, how the Commission can state that the alleged violation with supporting evidence and pressure the guilty party to enter into a conciliatory agreement.

Stage Four Example: Conciliation Agreement (CA) / Litigation
    In *FEC v. Colorado Republican Federal Campaign Committee* (S.C. 95-486), the FEC alleged a violation of expenditure and reporting regulations had been violated. The Colorado Republican Federal Campaign Committee challenged the constitutionality of 2 U.S.C. §441a(d) regarding the coordination and expenditure of funds. At the center of the dispute was the Colorado Republican Federal Campaign Committee's $15,000 radio advertisement about a state senatorial campaign. However, according to a complex formula concerning state party spending amounts in federal elections, the Committee is limited in the amount it could spend in the campaign. Under the FECA, the Colorado Republican Federal Campaign Committee can spend limited funds on coordinated party expenditures in connection with the general election campaign of the Republican Party candidate for the U.S. Senate from Colorado (2 U.S.C. §441a(d)). The Colorado Republican Federal Campaign Committee characterized the advertisement as a 'generic voter education expense' not subject to §441a(d) limits.
    U.S. District Court for the District of Colorado granted summary judgment to Colorado Republican Federal Campaign Committee (August 1993). The Tenth Circuit Court of Appeals, however, reversed the district court ruling (June 1995). On appeal the U.S. Supreme Court on June 26, 1996 ruled that the coordinated party expenditure limits at 2 U.S.C. §441a(d) do not apply to the radio advertisements. In addition, the Court ruled that the advertisement is an independent expenditure

and not subject expenditure limit. The Court vacated the 10th Circuit's decision and remanded the case for further review in light of this decision. Many campaign finance experts and court watchers believed that the final deposition of this case in 2000 weakened the extent to which the FEC can aggressively enforce the campaign finance laws.

Summary Comments

It is important to note that during its early years, the FEC did maintain a staff of legal investigators. Originally, this team of would conduct individual interviews and site visits as part of an investigation into possible FECA violations. However, within a year of the FEC starting its regulatory activities, administrative re-structuring and shifts in agency resources effectively disbanded this team. With the dissolution of the investigation team, the FEC now conducts enforcement investigations mostly through constrained formal interviews, depositions, and audits (Jackson 1990). Some see this as a major shortcoming of the agency to enforce the law (Weiser and McAllister 1997). Table 5.1 presents information illustrating FEC administrative enforcement trends over time.

Table 5.1.   Number of MURs Opened, 1975-2000

Year	#Opened	Change	Year	#Opened	Change
1975	57	0	1988	236	-25
1976	107	+228	1989	218	-18
1977	133	+90	1990	195	-23
1978	481	+348	1991	257	+62
1979	268	-213	1992	260	+3
1980	255	-13	1993	119	-141
1981	112	-143	1994	342	+223
1982	95	-17	1995	177	-165
1983	127	+32	1996	314	+137
1984	283	+156	1997	147	-167
1985	257	-26	1998	168	+21
1986	191	-66	1999	118	-50
1987	261	+70	2000	195	+77

Source: *Federal Election Commission Annual Reports* (1975-2000).

A review of this data presents interesting information regarding the administrative behavior of the FEC over time. First, during the early period of the FEC when it had the ability to conduct random audits and visits, the annual number of enforcement cases (MURs) opened swelled until revocation of this random audit power with the 1979 FECA Amendments. In addition, during this period, the FEC had its dedicated staff of enforcement investigators later disbanded. Second, during the Reagan presidency of the 1980's, we see a more subdued pattern of opening enforcement investigation. This more subdued enforcement behavior may have been a response to Reagan's mandate to reduce the size of government. Third, as the 1990s we see the annual trend of MUR opened fluctuate greatly, possibly responding to increased special interest activity and the use of new fundraising techniques. It was during this period that new uses of campaign finances in the form of soft money and issue advocacy advertisements play a more significant role in campaigns and elections.

Given its limited resources, the FEC recognized that it could not enforce the law effectively if it continued to handle every enforcement matter that came before it as if they were all similar in importance and scope. Consequently, the FEC now uses an Enforcement Prioritization System to focus on those cases that deserve special attention. Under this system, the FEC ranks enforcement cases according to specific criteria, and assigns only the more significant cases to staff. In addition, this process allows the FEC to dismiss cases that fall into two categories: low-rated cases (cases that do not warrant use of the agency's resources to pursue because of the cases lower significance relative to other pending matters) and stale cases (those that initially received a higher rating but remained unassigned for a significant period due to a lack of investigative resources).

Conclusion

This chapter provided an overview of the FEC and the agency's ability to administrate and enforce federal campaign finance law. This brief review of the FEC and its administrative and enforcement procedures established that staff must navigate through a labyrinth of enforcement procedures that are not only time consuming, but also places a heavy demand on agency resource. To understand how political officials may influence the agency's initiation of MUR, nonetheless, requires an analysis of the agency's relationship with political officials. The following chapter provides a review of the literature concerning this political-administrative relationship and resources officials use to influence FEC administrative behavior.

Chapter VI

The Political-Administrative Relationship

Woodrow Wilson (1887) suggested administrative agencies operate more business-like in order to enhance government effectiveness and efficiency. Wilson also asked whether politics and administration are separate functions, and how to maintain administrative accountability. Since these comments, the literature studying political-administrative relationships has evolved. First, classic studies of public administrative agency implementation of policy use general observations to analyze the relationship between politicians and administrative organizations include Goodnow (1900), Barnard (1938), Appleby (1949), Downs (1967), and Tullock (1965). These classic works note that many conflicting contextual forces—political in nature—influence the manner in which an administrative agency implements policy (Mosher 1976). Second, contemporary scholars increasingly using sophisticated statistical tools and methodology to analyze the causes and consequences of policy implementation include Stigler (1971), Peltzman (1976), Page (1985), Hamman (1993), Wood and Waterman (1994) Ringquist (1995), Scott (1997) and Corder (1998). This literature notes agency implementation of policy influenced by factors such as information asymmetries (Banks and Weingast 1992), monitoring mechanisms (McCubbins, Noll, and Weingast 1985, 1989), structural incentives (Macey 1992), agency design (Goodin 1996), and electoral incentives (Mayhew 1974). Overall though, it is important to recognize that much of this work concerning policy implementation is based on one of two predominate explanations of political-administrative relationships.

The current literature identifies *administrative autonomy* and *political control* as the two leading explanations of administrative behavior within the context of a political-administrative relationship. The administrative autonomy explanation of administrative behavior contends that politicians are not only uninterested in the actions of bureaucratic agencies, but also unable to influence policy administration and implementation. The administrative autonomy explanation maintains that incumbent elected officials pay little attention to administrative oversight and procedural review due to their preoccupation with re-election efforts (Dodd and Schott 1986). Other scholars believe that government administrative agencies have a great deal of autonomy in their interactions with political officials due to the policy expertise and information asymmetries that agencies enjoy over their hierarchical superiors (Niskanen 1971; Banks and Weingast 1992).

The political control explanation of administrative behavior claims that politicians influence administrative policy implementation to a significant degree. This research uses a principal-agent paradigm to show how elected officials influence administrative agencies using monitoring devices (i.e., Federal Register publications, public hearings, special committee reports) and an incentive (i.e., annual budget, legislation, political appointments, favorable judicial rulings) (Pfeffer and Salancik 1978; Moe 1984; Calvert, McCubbins, and Weingast 1989; McCubbins, Noll and Weingast 1990; Wood and Waterman 1994). Early studies based on this principal-agent explanation of the political-administrative relationship asserts that strong electoral incentives are the primary motivator for elected officials to become actively engaged in matters of policy administration to enhance their re-election possibilities (Mayhew 1974; Fiorina 1982). While the principal-agent explanation is valuable regarding analysis of the political-administrative relationship, it is worth noting its use comes under increasing scrutiny (Worsham, Eisner, and Ringquist 1997).

Any single explanation of how government organizations implement policy in the context of a political-administrative relationship, therefore, probably resides somewhere between the administrative autonomy and political control ideal-types (Barnard 1938; Simon 1957; Williamson 1996). While the use of such ideal-types is useful toward listing various theoretical explanations, it is also necessary to state and appreciate their value and limitations. The practical nature of political-administrative interaction, even so, dictates that this relationship is hierarchical with institutional officials having more power relative to organizational decision-makers regarding administrative arrangements, to include organizational resources and their use. The research collectively contends that to appreciate the complexity of policy-making and implementation in the context of a political-administrative relationship, attention should focus on how structural and managerial arrangements might influence administrative behavior over time (Mayhew 1974; Weingast 1984; Fisher 1993). Consequently, based on the theoretical framework and the relevant literature already discussed, we can now develop and present testable hypotheses that analyze relevant FEC data and produce findings which contribute to the scholarly fields of public administration, democratic theory, and organizational studies. First, it is necessary to clarify important terms and concepts used in the analysis regarding FEC enforcement and administration arrangements.

How a MUR Represents Agency Enforcement

Before discussing what constitutes a "matter-under-review," we must clarify its substantive value and delineate it from other symbolic enforcement actions the FEC might take. A MUR is an actual enforcement case opened by the FEC to investigate possible violation of the law. Therefore, initiation of a MUR is a substantive activity by the FEC to promote compliance with the law (Gross and Hong 1998). A MUR corresponds to the expected punishment in deterrence theory (i.e., the likelihood of being guilty of violating the law compounded by the expected value of the punishment if found guilty of violating the law) (Scholz and Pinney 1995). The FEC can also use symbolic enforcement activities to promote compliance with the law. Symbolic politics theory states that individuals engage in symbolic activity rather than substantive activity to manipulate others into perceiving that they are carrying out the public will (Edelman 1971; Hoerrner 1999).

Symbolic enforcement activities by the FEC may include "conciliation agreements" (agreements between the FEC and those found guilty of violating federal campaign finance law) and "request-for-additional-information" (agency requests to party committee concerning questionable campaign records). "Conciliation agreements" represent after-the-fact enforcement actions and not tactical agency action. "Request-for-additional-information" is not an actual enforcement action, as it does not entail formal punishment (Scholz 1991; Scholz and Pinney 1995). In addition, because departmental auditors or legal staff at the FEC can initiate this symbolic enforcement, its use in this analysis would be inappropriate. Thus a MUR, as opposed to "conciliation agreements" or "requests-for-additional-information," represents (a) real agency enforcement that (b) requires substantial resource toward its implementation and is (c) substantive punishment for violators. To capture this dynamic, the analysis uses the difference in annual number of MUR cases opened by the FEC from 1976 through 2000 to measure changes the agency's administrative behavior. MUR data are the change in actual enforcement cases opened by the FEC to investigate possible violations of the law.

The following data represent symbolic enforcement efforts of the FEC over time. Figure 6.1 (Annual Number of "Conciliation Agreements") compares the annual number of "conciliation agreements" with the 'dollar amount' (thousands of dollars) collected through civil penalties negotiated from 1985 through 2000. It is important to note that between 1993 and 1994 the FEC significantly increased the dollar amounts for civil penalties paid in regards to a "conciliation agreement." This accounts for the exaggerated spike in Figure 6.1 for the noted period. The FEC might enhance the quality of this data by providing more substantive information concerning the different types of agreements that the agency reaches over time.

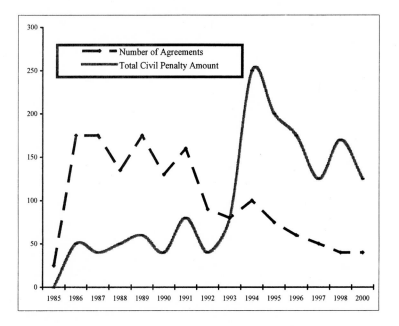

Figure 6.1.   Symbolic Enforcement, 1985-2000.
Source: *Federal Election Commission Annual Reports* (1975-2000).

Definitions and Limitations

It is necessary to state the precise operational definitions of terms used frequently in the course of the analysis, beginning with general descriptive terms. "Administrative behavior" in the context of this research represents FEC initiation of enforcement cases known as a "matters-under-review" or MUR. Using annual change in the number of MUR initiated by the FEC is a good measure of the agency's administrative behavior for the following reasons. First, initiation of a MUR represents the central enforcement function of the FEC. Second, initiation of a MUR accurately represents the resource-based nature of FEC enforcement activities. Third, initiation of a MUR is a substantive enforcement activity that entails real punishment for violators. In addition, the term "political officials" represents Congress, the president, and the Supreme Court. Finally, the term "resources" represents those items supplied by political officials that are (a) necessary and sufficient for the operation of the agency and (b) non-replaceable.

Independent variables used also require defining. The budget variable is the annual change in FEC budget from the previous year as determined through annual budgetary processes that provides the agency with the fiscal resources necessary for it to accomplish its regulatory duties. The legislation variable is defined as federal legislation passed by Congress and signed into law by the president that either changes federal campaign finance law or involves the FEC in its administration. The appointment variable is the initial appointment of an FEC Commissioner. The judicial variable is the Supreme Court's actions concerning consideration or review of campaign finance related cases. While the above variable definitions and concepts are open to criticism, they nonetheless provide a meaningful starting point for analysis.

Hypotheses

The literature discusses the importance of administrative structure and management regarding political-administrative relationships pertaining to policy implementation. The following sections present testable hypotheses that address the nature of political-administrative relationships specifically regarding the FEC. Because the FEC uses managerial resources such as annual budget, legislation, appointments, and judicial actions according to structural procedures to administrate and enforce the law, examining how political officials manipulate these arrangements is important (Sabatier and Mazmanian 1979; Donaldson 1996). The literature notes agency resources and procedures as important contingency factors regarding administrative response to political influence (Fenno 1966; Wilson 1989; Donaldson 1996; Krause 1996).

Before proceeding, a note about expectations of hypotheses and their testing is necessary. The development and test of the following hypotheses is an attempt to draw general inferences from available public data and literary accounts since social science can never prove anything in a strict scientific sense. To this end, the development and presentation of hypotheses regarding administrative behavior and their relevance to political official and the FEC relationships is offered. The analysis measures relationships that might exist between identified independent and dependent variables and assess the correlation between the two when necessary and understood accordingly. This analysis, therefore, provides data describing possible relationships between selected various organization-level variables from 1975 through 2000. Interpretation the data, as with all research, is vulnerable to criticism that question assumptions and methodology.

Annual Agency Budget
    A number of studies contend that presidential and congressional fiscal decisions influence administrative behavior through budgetary measures (Bendor and Moe 1985; Scholz and Wei 1986; Carpenter 1996). Specifically, when a budget sets spending boundaries according to particular purposes, it becomes a tool for political officials in government to influence agency action (Wildavsky 1972, 1988). Consequently, agency budget is an independent variable reflecting the joint preferences of the president and Congress with regard to administrative behavior (Kiewiet and McCubbins 1988, 1991). This is of particular importance in the case of the FEC in light of the fact that the agency has a concurrent budget given to executive and legislative budgetary officials for review. It is reasonable to assume that FEC initiation of MURs over time should have a positive relationship to annual increases in agency budgets due to the agency's use of additional fiscal resources to engage in additional enforcement activities. Because the budget is necessary for agency resources ranging from staff to staplers, it is important to understand how annual fiscal changes might influence agency enforcement actions. This leads to the first hypothesis of the research:

> Hypothesis 1: There is a positive relationship between annual change in agency budget and annual agency initiation of MURs from 1976 to 2000.

Analyzing annual changes in agency budget—adjusted for inflation—provides insight into how political officials might influence FEC administrative behavior. Concerning the budget variable, it is necessary to outline the procedures and reasoning justifying its use in this research. First, the budget data used are the actual amount appropriated by Congress following budget recommendations from the Office of Management and Budget (OMB), House Appropriation and Senate Appropriation committee hearings. Second, the data are the CPI Index listed in the *Statistical Abstract of the United States* (1999). Third, this data reflects annual budgetary data changes to capture the dynamic nature of FEC funding. This creates a budgetary variable that reflects fiscal changes adjusted for inflationary pressure. Finally, note that historically Congress earmarks significant portions of the agency's budget for specific activities such as technological upgrades. The budget data used in this analysis includes these annual amounts due to the theoretical problem of discerning if budgetary earmark amounts are or are not effectively related to agency enforcement efforts.

Campaign Finance Legislation

Researchers contend strong electoral incentives motivate legislators to introduce or advocate particular public policies that support their electoral or philosophical interests (Truman 1959; Ferejohn and Shipan 1990; Krebhbiel 1991; Horn 1995). Specifically, political officials may introduce legislation to inhibit vigorous enforcement of campaign finance law by the FEC (Mayhew 1974; Fiorina 1982; Weingast 1984). Because Congress and the president have the ability to promulgate and enact legislation that may "thicken" an agency's administrative processes, it is important to understand the relationship between legislation and FEC initiation of MUR (Moe 1982; Light 1995). It is then reasonable to assume that FEC initiation of MURs over time might have a negative relationship with changes about federal campaign finance law because policy changes will either restrict enforcement activity or require new administrative processes for their implementation. Enactment of legislation that expands FEC duties in such a manner is important because this places an even greater demand on the use of already scarce agency resources (e.g., "overload). This leads to the second hypothesis:

> Hypothesis 2: There is a negative relationship between congressional enactment of new campaign finance law and annual agency initiation of MURs from 1976 to 2000.

A four-point ordinal scale is used to measure how enactment or the amendment of campaign finance is associated with legislation that influences FEC initiation of MURs, using the following coding criteria and distinctions: 0 = no legislative change; 1= minor legislative change; 2 = moderate legislative change; and 3= major legislative change. No legislative change represents any major legislative action has taken by Congress for that year.

Minor legislative change signifies that FEC behavior does not shift despite enacted legislation. An example of minor legislative change is the *Ethics Reform Act Amendments of 1989* (P.L. 101-194). This Act changed several elements related to federal elections such as (a) repeal of the "Grandfather Clause" that permitted retiring Members of Congress to convert excess campaign funds to personal use and (b) new requirements that all incumbent and non-incumbents candidates for Congress file their personal finance reports with the FEC. This legislation either does or does not impose additional administrative duties on the FEC.

Moderate legislative change signifies that FEC behavior shifted substantively due to enacted legislative change. An example of moderate legislative change is the *House-Point-of-Entry Act of 1996* (P.L. 104-79) legislation. Before the enactment of this legislation, members of the House of Representatives would file campaign disclosure reports with the Clerk of the House who would make this information available to the public. However, because of the 1996 legislation, the FEC now has complete administrative responsibility for the intake, filing, and public accessibility of this information.

Major legislative change signifies a complete shift in FEC behavior due to the enacted legislation. An example of major legislative change is the *Federal Election Campaign Act Amendments of 1979* (P.L. 96-187). Following the 1976 and 1978 elections, amendments to the FECA (a) simplified reporting requirements (b) encouraged party building efforts (c) increased the public funding for presidential nominating conventions and (d) repealed FEC random audit ability (Table 6.1).

It is important, however, to note that despite the rigor of the analysis the ability to completely capture and measure the influence legislative change has on administration behavior is beyond our ability to measure and interpret precisely over time. To some extend, regardless of the empirical findings of this analysis, we will most likely not be completely satisfied with the findings and will have to rely, to some degree, on a less precise but much richer contextual analysis to more completely address the relevant hypothesis.

Table 6.1.   Federal Campaign Finance Legislation, 1976-2000

Year	Legislation	Public Law
1976	FECA Amendments	(P.L. 94-283)
1979	FECA Amendments	(P.L. 96-187)
1981	FEC Authorization (Reorganization)	(P.L. 93-253)
1989	Ethics Reform Act Amendments	(P.L. 101-194)
1993	Presidential Fund (Omnibus Budget)	(P.L. 103-66)
1994	National Voter Registration Act of 1993	(P.L. 103-31)
1996	House Point-of-Entry	(P.L. 104-79)

Source: *Federal Election Commission Annual Reports* (1975-2000).

Political Appointments

Third, research on political appointments focus on the consequence of organizational leadership to maintain administrative autonomy that is derived from information asymmetries the agency may have in relationship to political officials (Niskanen 1971, 1994; Banks and Weingast 1992). However, regulatory agencies may not enjoy the same information advantage over lawmakers that other administrative agencies may have due to managerial procedures, legislative oversight, and reporting requirements. Other scholars contend that administrative behavior is primarily the result of organizational leadership expertise and professionalism (Peters 1984; Meier 1987; Wilson 1989; Eisner and Meier 1990; Bawn 1995). Research focusing on the relationship between political appointees and administrative behavior show that organizational leadership is critical to agency implementation of policy (Niskanen 1994; Banks and Weingast 1992). In addition, research indicates that new political appointees reduce administrative effectiveness due to their political ties to officeholders and lack of specialized training for appointed positions (Koven 1994). Appointment of new commissioners to the FEC should have a negative relationship with the annual number of MUR opened. This leads to the third hypothesis:

> Hypothesis 3: There is a negative relationship between the appointment of new FEC Commissioners and annual agency's initiation of MURs from 1976 to 2000.

The appointment variable represents the annual number of initial appointments made to the Commission. Regarding the appointment variable, it is necessary to comment on its use and interpretation in this research. Typically, political appointments inform us about the political ideology and motives of the president. However, FEC appointments are unique when compared to other regulatory agencies for two reasons. First, according to the FECA, the FEC must have a politically balanced commission of three Republicans and three Democrats. Thus, having a politically balanced commission means that neither partisan interest has a voting majority. Second, it is customary that the initial selection of possible appointees does not come from the president, but instead from Republican and Democratic leadership. It is customary that, party leadership submits a list of names to the President for consideration. Figure 6.2 presents appointment data that illustrate the sometime unusual pattern of FEC appointment activity.

Table 6.2.   FEC Appointments, 1976-2000

Name	Appointment Date	Re-Appointment Date
Aikens, Joan (R)	1975*	1976, 1981, 1983, 1989
Curtis, Thomas (R)	1975*	na
Harris, Thomas (D)	1975*	1976, 1979
Staebler, Neil (D)	1975*	1976*
Thomson, Vernon (R)	1975*/81	1976/81
Tiernan, Robert (D)	1976*	1976
Springer, William (R)	1976	na
McGarry, John (D)	1978	1983, 1989
Friedersdorf, Max (R)	1979	na
Reiche, Frank (R)	1979	na
Elliott, Lee Ann (R)	1981	1987, 1994
McDonald, Danny (D)	1981	1987, 1994
Josefiak, Thomas (R)	1985	na
Thomas, Scott (D)	1986	1991
Potter, Trevor (R)	1991	na
Mason, David (R)	1998	na
Sandstrom, Karl (D)	1998	na
Wold, Darryl (R)	1998	na
Smith, Bradley (D)	2000	na

Note: *Initial appointment 1976 used (re-constitution of FEC).
Source: *Federal Election Commission Annual Reports* (1975-2000).

Supreme Court Actions

Although the Supreme Court does not have direct authority over the FEC similar to that of Congress or the president, its unique relationship to government organizations allows it to influence policy implementation (Shapiro 1968; Melnick 1983; Smith 1993; James 1996). Shapiro's (1968) seminal work on the Supreme Court's relationship with administrative agencies contends that the relationship between the Supreme Court and administrative agencies is in part political (Katzmann 1980; Canon and Johnson 1984). Stated more directly, FEC and the Supreme Court relationship while different from relationships between the FEC and Congress or the president is nonetheless political (Shapiro 1968). This statement is not an attempt to tarnish the reputation of the nation's highest court, but only recasting what the referenced literature already concludes, and thereby properly frames this relationship. This critique of the relationship between the FEC and the Supreme Court, therefore, highlights the political nature of their interaction.

The Court might express its support or non-support for FEC regulatory activities in its actions concerning campaign finance related cases (Wood and Waterman 1994; Spriggs 1996). It therefore seems reasonable to assume that FEC initiation of MUR over time responds to Supreme Court actions in cases concerning campaign finance law (Canon and Johnson 1984). Specifically, actions by the Supreme Court concerning federal election policy, either favoring the FEC or not, force FEC decision-makers to reevaluate the legal implications of the Courts actions. Following the Court's action in cases involving campaign finance law, legal uncertainty lessens. Thus, the Court's actions should have a positive relationship with FEC initiate of MUR. This leads to the fourth hypothesis of the research:

> Hypothesis 4: There is a positive relationship between Supreme Court action in cases involving federal campaign finance law and annual agency initiation of MURs from 1976 to 2000.

A four-point ordinal scale is used to measure how judicial action by the Supreme Court in cases concerning campaign finance law are associated with FEC initiation of MUR using the following coding criteria and distinctions: 0 = no judicial change; 1 = minor judicial change; 2 = moderate judicial change; and 3 = major judicial change. No judicial change represents agency behavior remaining the same when there is no Supreme Court judicial action.

Minor judicial change by the Court influences FEC enforcement activity is characterized as insignificant. This would usually apply to cases in which the Court concurs with the Commission's position. An example of minor judicial change is the case of *Democratic Senatorial Campaign Committee v. FEC* (1981). In this case, the Democratic Senatorial Campaign Committee sought a declaration from the Court that the "no reason to believe" finding in an earlier case the FEC reviewed violated expenditure provisions of the FECA concerning various Republican Senatorial candidates in 1978 was contrary to the law and ordered the Commission to comply with the declaration within 30 days. The Supreme Court granted FEC petition for a *writ of certiorari* in this case and the agency prevailed.

Moderate judicial change signifies a substantive change to FEC enforcement policy due to judicial action, usually in cases that the Court does not concur with the agency's position. An example of moderate judicial change is the case of the *FEC v. Political Contributions Data* (1994). In this case, following Political Contributions Data victory over the FEC in the Court of Appeals concerning its right to sale contributor lists published by the FEC, Political Contributions Data applied to the district court for an award of attorneys' fees and other expenses pursuant to the Equal Access to Justice Act. For judicial consideration, an application for attorney's fees filed within 30 days of the date the judgment has become final. While the district court contended a judgment is final when the losing party asserts no further appeal will occur, the U.S. Court of Appeals for the Second Circuit found that Political Contributions Data filed its application for attorneys' fees within 30 days of the final judgment as required under the Equal Access to Justice Act. The basis for this finding is that the date of final judgment was the last day the FEC could have applied for a *writ of certiorari* with the Supreme Court. On February 22, 1994, the Supreme Court denied an FEC petition to review the appellate court judgment and was required to pay Political Contributions Data's attorneys. The Solicitor General, who filed a friend of the court brief supporting the FEC petition, said the Court's finding in this case expands FEC liability for attorney fees.

Major judicial change signifies a substantive and momentous change to FEC enforcement policy due to judicial action, usually in cases that the Court not only disagrees with the agency's position, but also provides judicial opinions that cast doubt upon government efforts to regulate campaign finances. An example of major judicial change is the case of *Buckley v. Valeo* (1976). In this case, the constitutionality of the 1974 FECA Amendments challenged. The major finding of this case was that the Court upheld the 1974 FECA contribution limit provisions but overturned its expenditure limit provisions. Acknowledging both contribution and spending limits had First Amendment implications, the Court stated that the 1974 FECA Amendments' expenditure limits impose significantly more severe restrictions on protected freedoms of political expression and relationship than do its limitations on financial contributions. The Court, nevertheless, contended that expenditure limits placed on publicly funded candidates were constitutional because presidential candidates were free to disregard the limits if they chose to reject the public financing. Serious debate considering overturning this case and the Court's findings continues. All cases considered or reviewed by the Supreme Court concerning campaign finance law are cases in which the FEC is directly or indirectly related. It should be noted that the majority of the identified cases address constitutional and communication matters (Table 6.3).

Table 6.3.   Selected Supreme Court Cases, 1976-2000

Supreme Court Case	Case Number & Date
Buckley v. Valeo	424 U.S. 1(1976)
First Nat. Bank of Boston v. Bellotti	435 U.S. 765(1978)
RNC v. FEC	445 U.S. 955(1980)
Nat. Chamber Alliance Politics v. FEC	449 U.S. 954(1980)
DSCC v. FEC	454 U.S. 27(1981)
Calif. Medical Relationship v. FEC	453 U.S. 182(1981)
Common Cause v. Schmitt	455 U.S. 129(1982)
FEC v. Nat. Right to Work Committee	459 U.S. 197(1982)
Bread PAC v. FEC	455 U.S. 577(1984)
Athens Lumber Co. v. FEC	465 U.S. 1092(1984)
FEC v. NCPAC	470 U.S. 480(1985)
FEC v. Mass. Citizens for Life	479 U.S. 238(1986)
Austin v. MI State Chamber of Comm.	494 U.S. 652(1990)
FEC v. Political Contribution Data	943 F2d 190(2d Cir 1991)(1994)
FEC v. NRA Political Victory Fund	115 S. Ct. 537(1994)
FEC v. Colorado RFCC	116 S. Ct. 2309(1996)
FEC v. Williams	118 S. Ct. 600(1997)
Maine Right to Life v. FEC	118 S. Ct. 52(1997)
Clifton v. FEC	118 S. Ct. 1036(1998)
FEC v. Akins	118 S. Ct. 1777(1998)

Source: *FEC Selected Court Case Abstracts, 1976-2000* (2000).

Methodology

To analysis the relationship between the administrative behavior of the FEC and political officials, two kinds of information are gathered and analyzed. First, there is the collection and analysis of qualitative information. The research uses a case study approach to examine this information about the relationship between the FEC and political officials in 1998. Selection of this particular data is according to the belief that examining the FEC-political official relationship during this period highlights the dynamic and difficult nature of administrating and enforcing a public policy in an intense political environment. While this data does not produce results that are as certain as those arrived at using statistical analysis, it does embed the analysis within the historical context of the phenomena of interest it provides a more realistic assessment than a straightforward statistical analysis.

Second, there is the collection and analysis of quantitative data. The analysis uses statistical graphs of longitudinal data regarding the relationship between FEC administrative behavior and several independent variables (i.e., budget, legislation, appointment, and judicial action) (see Tufte 1983). This approach provides more certain information as to allow for the assessment of testable hypotheses presented in the pervious chapter. The analysis provides antidotal and empirical information that provides a realistic assessment of an important political-administrative relationship that may directly or indirectly determine of policy outcomes are consistent or not with democratic theory and government. As King, Keohane, and Verba (1994) note "...nonstatistical research will produce more reliable results if researchers pay attention to the rules of scientific inference" (p.6) (Morton 1999).

Finally, this analysis maintains the validity and reliability required of formal research. First, all data are valid measures of political and administrative actions as they accurately represent what they intend to measure. MUR is an actual measure of the FEC efforts to enforcement of the law. Budget, legislation, appointment, and judicial action are actual measures for the concepts they represent. In addition, all quantifiable data and measurements used in this analysis come from various public collections and reports collected from various official federal agencies and offices of the United States Government. Second, all data and measurements used in this analysis are reliable measures of political officials' actions and FEC administrative behavior because of their consistent use as such during the period under review. Standards for identifying enforcement cases, annual budget, legislation, appointments, and judicial action are consistent measures over time and readily verifiable.

Conclusion

This chapter reviewed the literature concerning the political-administrative relationship. In general, the literary record indicates that a variety of explanations concerning the political-administrative relationships develop over time. While early pioneers of this field examine these types of relationships using qualitative methodologies, contemporary researchers attempt to expand the analysis by using more quantitative and statistical techniques. Cumulatively then, this literature notes that political officials have at their disposal budgetary, legislative, appointment, and judicial tools to influence administrative behavior. Finally, this chapter also presented the methodological approach the research uses to analyze the relationships between FEC initiation of a MUR, and multiple independent variables such as agency budget, legislation, appointments, and judicial actions from 1976 to 2000. The following chapter provides an analysis that combines qualitative and quantitative research methodologies. Justification for using a mixed research design is to provide the broadest possible analysis to best understand the relationship between FEC administrative behavior and political officials' actions regarding manipulation of agency resources and administrative arrangements.

Chapter VII

An Analysis of the FEC-Political Relationship

At first glance, 1998 does not appear to provide a good case for analyzing relationships between the FEC and political officials concerning the administration and enforcement of federal campaign finance law. In fact, on a number of points, it seems that an analysis of this political-administrative relationship should provide ample evidence of the FEC perhaps asserting itself more forcefully in the face of political pressure. First, macro-level political factors appear to produce a general atmosphere of stability. The overall economic health of the United States was at an all-time high with the stock market producing records on a seemingly daily basis. Gross domestic product (GDP) continues to increase as both the public and private sectors prepare to meet the challenge posed by possible change of the century difficulties. Second, the national employment picture was the best it has ever been in the past ten years as average annual unemployment remained at or about 4.5% (Bureau of Labor Statistics, 2000). Third, while numerous domestic and foreign policy challenges remain on policy-makers' agenda, there was no single large-scale policy crisis.

Although these and other macro-level factors seem to indicate a relatively stable political environment in 1998 for the FEC, nevertheless, micro-level turmoil put the agency in the center of a political maelstrom. Specifically, that during 1998 political partisanship not only took root in Washington, but threatened government's overall ability to function effectively. The partisan politics experienced in Washington during 1998 had the potential to produce policy outcomes that might align more closely to the desires of the few rather than the many.

The Political Environment of 1998

At the center of the political turmoil during 1998 was the battle between a highly partisan Republican controlled Congress and a two-term incumbent Democratic president. In an intense partisan context, the U.S. House of Representatives in December 1998 approved two articles of impeachment accusing President Clinton of perjury and obstruction of justice. At issue is whether the President lied under oath about a sexual relationship with a former White House intern that extend from earlier questions about sexual harassment charges brought by another woman against him.

President Clinton denied any involvement with the White House intern, even going so far as to make a public statement on national television to that effect. Following the initial denial by President Clinton, come months of legalistic stalling by his legal advisors. Nonetheless, President Clinton, pressured by Independent Counsel Kenneth Starr, submitted to a four hours videotape testimony session. Despite President Clinton's equivocates on numerous points, he does admit to having had an "inappropriate" relationship with the White House intern. Although finally admitting to the indiscretion, President Clinton denies lying to the Special Counsel or abusing his power. As the media focused on official investigations, hostility between the President and his Republican accusers was raised to epic proportions.

After impeachment by the House of Representatives, Clinton vows to remain in office for the duration of his second term and appeals for a bipartisan compromise when the Senate begins the trial stage of the impeachment process. Although the President escaped removal from office, it is clear the bitter partisanship publicly displayed in 1998 underlines a real and significant divide between the actions of government and public opinion. While this matter defies quantitative analysis, antidotal accounts of this matter seem to support the belief that these actions had a negative influence on government operations and general political efficacy.

Data in Table 7.1 illustrates how divided the American public was over this issue and hints about its feelings concerning relationships between the executive and legislative branches of the federal government. This information underscores the apparent disconnect between public opinion and the actions of political officials. That is, along with illustrating the intense political climate of 1998 in Washington, D.C., this historic event exemplifies the widening gap between popular sentiment for particular government action and government's non-response to an identified public concern such as campaign finance reform.

Table 7.1.   Impeachment Polls: President Clinton: Scandals and
                  Investigations

Question: "Should the House of Representatives vote 'yes' or 'no' to
impeach the President and send him to trial in the Senate?"

	ALL	Men	Women
Yes	44%	47%	41%
No	52%	51%	54%
Not sure	4%	3%	6%

Question: "If the trial in the Senate were held today, should the Senate
vote to remove the President or keep him in office?"

	ALL	Men	Women
Remove him	35%	38%	33%
Keep him	59%	57%	61%
Not	6%	6%	6%

Data are from nationwide surveys of Americans 18 & older conducted November-December, 1998. N=1,003 likely voters nationwide.
Source: Zogby International. *America Poll*. December 10-13, 1998.

Specifically, popular sentiment is that campaign finance regulations are not protecting the legitimacy of democratic campaigns and elections in the United States (Table 7.2). Underlying the public's attitude about money in politics is the belief that the FEC is not capable of providing adequate levels administration and enforcement to match the public's expectations. One reason for gap between expectation and performance might be (a) unrealistic expectations about campaign finance regulation and (b) incompatibility between administrative arrangements and organizational demands. For instance, due to resource and administrative limitations, the FEC can only assign the equivalent of 24 attorneys to its pending caseload no matter how large the caseload (e.g., 162 cases involving over 1,500 respondents as of March 1998). In addition, the number of respondents in administrative complaints reported to the FEC is growing. While the average pending caseloads in 1995 and 1997 remained the same, the number of respondents in those cases went from 1,636 in 1995 to 2,039 in 1997—a 25 percent increase. Part of this expansion had to do with the increased complexity of recent court decisions such as *FEC v. NRA Political Victory Fund* and *FEC v. Colorado Republican Federal Campaign Com-*

mittee. The US Supreme Court decision in *FEC v. Colorado Republican Federal Campaign Committee* forced FEC staffers to review all pervious enforcement cases (from 1976 to 1997) to protect against possible past violation of FECA statutes concerning coordination of contributions (*The Record,* May 1998). As the data illustrate, partisan politics and legal complexities lead to a situation at the FEC in which implementation of a public policy is limited.

Table 7.2.   Importance of Campaign Finance Reform (by Party)

Question:"How important will reforming election campaign finance laws be to you in deciding how to vote in the 2000 presidential election in November—very important, somewhat important, not too important, or not important at all?"

Party	Very Important	Somewhat Important	Not Too Important	Not Important At All	Don't Know
Democrat	40%	41%	12%	5%	2%
Republican	27%	29%	23%	18%	2%
Independent	35%	39%	16%	7%	3%
All	34%	36%	16%	11%	3%

Washington Post National Telephone Survey (March 30-April 2, 2000) N=1,083.
Source: Campaign Finance. (2001). *Public Agenda* [Online]. Available: http://www.publicagenda.org/issues [2001, October 3].

Ramifications for the FEC
    Analysis of partisan politics provides important information concerning the broad question of why the nature of a public policy matters when considering how political-administrative relationships influence policy outcomes in the context of democratic government. First, the significant events of 1998 provide an excellent case study for analyzing how political turmoil disrupts the normal course of the policy-making process. With so much of the energy and resources of Congress going into what some might describe as one individual's moral failing rather than a constitutional crisis, little time is left for Congress to consider matters that were not of immediate significance. Other than routine budgetary, administrative, and representative functions, Congress as an institution, while not coming to a complete stop does appear to slow considerable while diverting federal dollars to scandal-related matters. For instance, the final expenditure for Special Prosecutor Kenneth

Starr's office for the Clinton investigations totaled $52 million (GAO/AIMD-00-283R, August 2000). Regardless of the final dollar amount, media and political commentators on both sides of this ideological battle contend the actual cost of the investigation is much higher when considering "opportunity costs." Missed "opportunity costs" might include legislators' inability to tackle other long-term policy issues critical to the economic, political, and national security. Some of the issues Congress and the Administration are unable to sufficiently address in 1998 due in part to the ongoing presidential investigation and impeachment proceedings include energy policy, education reform, military preparedness, immigration screening, foreign relationships, terrorism, and campaign finance reform. While there is no way of knowing if Congress or the Administration would have addressed these and other policy issues more intensely if not for the ongoing presidential investigations, there is little doubt that the impeachment investigation did place additional pressure on already limited physical and human capital resources.

Second, and specifically to the matter of the FEC, both Republican and Democratic leadership during 1998 seem to advocate an FEC agenda that is restrained at best. For Republicans, with Democratic President Bill Clinton under unprecedented political and social pressure to resolve issues related to his personal indiscretions, the FEC finds itself at the mercy of a Republican controlled Congress that does not appear to support progressive or even moderate FEC activity. During 'normal' political periods, the FEC, like other regulatory agencies, can count on partisan forces in the executive and legislative branch principals to "check and balance" one another to prevent either from unduly abusing administrative agents. However, with the attention of the Democratic Party leadership focused on the continuing presidential scandal, the usual partisan "checks and balances" that provides the FEC some cover from intense political bias is absent.

With Republican control of the House and Senate during 1998, conservative leadership has the political advantage to influence FEC decision-makers in such a manner that the agency's activities parallel conservative views of extensive limited government. For Democrats, this means that new questions about the use of foreign funds in the 1996 Clinton-Gore re-election campaign effort are coming under closer public scrutiny. The Justice Department must determine if an independent counsel is necessary to investigate President Clinton, Vice President Al Gore and other Democratic officials concerning allegation of campaign spending violations. These allegations contend the Clinton-Gore team control of advertising paid for by the Democratic National Committee, and thereby circumventing the spending limits on individual federal campaigns. While Republicans and Democrats leadership might have seen limited FEC activity in 1998 as consistent with their own narrow political interests, regardless, public sentiment seems to reflect the opposite (see Table 7.2). The following sections provide empirical data over time illustrating the FEC-political official relationship over a 25-year period.

Budget

Data in Figure 7.1 provides the following information. At various points over time, we see two things: (a) significant increases in FEC annual budgets just before presidential elections; and (b) limited or even no increase in the agency's annual budgets between presidential elections and during mid-term campaigns. Therefore, while the data does seem to provide limited support for Hypothesis 1, it is clear that the budget numbers alone can not provide a complete picture of the proposed relationship between FEC annual enforcement activity and budgetary changes over time. Any improvement toward gaining a more complete explanation of this relationship requires an analysis of the actual budget process as it relates to the FEC.

The budget process is an annual event that generally does not provide dramatic shifts in funding. After adjusting for inflation, the annual FEC budget amounts appear to deviate from past funding patterns significantly. Due to the procedural nature of agency funding and the fact that the FEC must submit a concurrent budget to Congress and the president, the final dollar amount the FEC receives annually appears to lead to the conclusion that the relationship between FEC administrative behavior and the budget variable is at best minimal. The data indicate that there might be a slightly positive relationship between annual budget and the initiation of enforcement actions (e.g., MURs) over time. In addition, because of the president's budgetary recommendation and congressional oversight, FEC decision-makers remain constantly aware of how elected public officials might view agency enforcement activities. As part of the normal annual budget process, FEC administrators and appointed Commissioners must first, submit their fiscal year budget request to the executive branch OMB and the legislative branch Congressional Budget Office for review and comment. Next, the FEC must attend hearings before the House Administration Committee's Subcommittee on Elections, the House Appropriations' Subcommittee on Treasury, Postal Service & General Government, and the Senate's Committee on Rules & Administration. Perhaps due to the routine nature of this process, the data cannot show how political officials use the appropriations process to influence FEC administrative behavior. A cynical explanation for the existence of this proposed relationship is that any correlation between FEC enforcement actions and its annual budget is limited because the agency historically received inadequate funds to enforce federal campaign finance laws adequately. Based on the evidence, therefore, it seems that while there is limited evidence to support Hypothesis 1, additional qualitative analysis might uncover additional evidence to support the proposed relationship. Thus, the quantitative analysis provides cautious support for a positive relationship between agency budget and enforcement with the caveat that qualitative analysis is necessary to better provide a more complete and realistic picture of the proposed relationship. The following section offers just such an analysis.

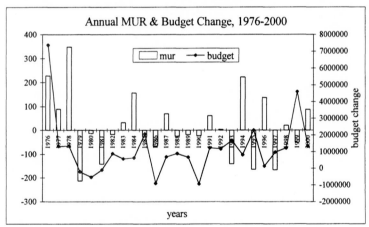

Figure 7.1.   MUR and FEC Budget, 1976-2000
Source: *Federal Election Commission Annual Reports* (1975-2000).

1998 FEC Budgeting

In 1998, Congress appropriated $31 million dollars to fund the FEC operation of which $750 thousand dollars earmarked for a Pricewaterhouse Coopers audit of the Commission's operations. As part of the Commission's FY 1998 appropriation, Congress earmarked $750,000 for an independent audit of the FEC Congress directed the GAO to contract for a technological and performance audit and management review of the FEC. At the time Congress requests the following "impartial assessments": (a) overall effectiveness of the FEC in meeting its statutory responsibilities; (b) the appropriateness and effectiveness of the FEC organizational structure, systems and performance measures for accomplishing its mission; (c) the adequacy of the agency's strategic information resource management plan as a tool for increasing FEC efficiency and effectiveness through the use of data processing systems; (d) adequacy of FEC human resource programs for obtaining and maintaining adequate staff expertise and organizational capacity; (e) the adequacy and completeness of internal management and financial controls systems to efficiently and effectively serve the FEC management needs and the reliability of information provided by these systems; and (f) the satisfaction of the regulated community with the products and services the FEC provides. More than $4 million of the remaining $30 million is set aside for specific non-personnel uses, yielding an operational budget of roughly $26 million. The bulk of the $4 million set-aside was devoted to computer enhancements, including $1.3 million for computerized litigation and enforcement document support. Although short of the Commission's request, the 313.5 FTE staffing authorization was an increase over the actual FY 1997 staffing level of 297 FTE (*FEC Annual Report*).

Also important at that time was that Representative Robert Livingston (R-LA) is preparing to become the next Speaker of the Republican controlled House. This is significant for various reasons. Livingston believed in drastically reducing the size of government in terms of resources and restraining government regulatory authority. As Chair of the House Appropriations Committee, Livingston proposed severe measures to curtail what he perceives as unrestrained government growth that presents a threat to individual freedom and liberties. As Appropriations Chair for the past four years, Livingston made a point of challenging the regulatory authority of the FEC, specifically questioning the agency's legitimacy to exist in the first place. In fact, during House Appropriation Hearing for the FY1995 FEC budget, Livingston attacked then Commission Chair Trevor Potter, not only regarding agency related budget matters, but also on a host of other issues administrative and enforcement issues (Potter and McDonald 1994). Thus, FEC decision-makers and staff are suspended in a perpetual state of uncertainty.

FY 1999 Budget (projected): In 1999, the FEC received the $37 million dollars FY 1999 appropriation that it requests. Congress, however, earmarked nearly $4.5 million dollars of this budget for computerization, and "fences" off more than $1 million, pending a Commis-

sion plan for the use of these funds. While Congress encouraged the
FEC to improve its enforcement program and practices, it stipulated
that the agency could not hire additional staff relating to it carrying out
its enforcement duties. Moreover, Congress set a 347 FTE cap on overall staffing, well below the agency's desire of 360 FTE. The agency
had hoped to increase its overall workforce to 360 FTE by adding 47
positions—37 of which would have been in compliance and enforcement. In March of the same year, FEC Vice Chairman Scott Thomas
testified in support of the Commission's staffing increase before the
House Appropriations Subcommittee on Treasury, Postal Service, and
General Government and argued that greater enforcement resources are
necessary for the agency to meet its enforcement responsibilities. Mr.
Thomas said it is imperative to have more and better skilled staff to
insure that FEC enforcement of campaign finance law is meaningful,
adding that without adequate staffing, the agency can not provide reliable disclosure and enforcement as illustrated in Tables 7.3 and 7.4
(*The Record*, July 1998).

Table 7.3 Functional Allocation of Budget, 1998-1999

Year	FY 1998 (actual)	FY1999 (projected)
Personnel	20,595,216	23,407,500
Travel / Transportation	195,538	947,500
Space Rental	2,509,470	3,251,000
Phones / Postage	497,966	515,412
Printing	277,242	330,205
Training / Tuition	96,584	304,395
Contracts / Services	2,326,013	3,940,210
Maintenance / Repairs	466,633	381,450
Software / Hardware	381,710	1,390,500
Federal Agency Service	1,102,782	1,713,550
Supplies	345,497	293,778
Publications	250,353	341,500
Equipment Purchases	1,130,979	633,000
Total	*30,175,983*	*36,850,000*

Source: *1998 FEC Annual Report*

Table 7.4 Allocation of Staff, 1998-1999

Year	FY 1998 (actual)	FY1999 (projected)
Commissioners	20,595,216	23,407,500
Inspector General	195,538	947,500
Staff Director	2,509,470	3,251,000
Administration	497,966	515,412
Audit	277,242	330,205
Information	96,584	304,395
Clearinghouse	2,326,013	3,940,210
Office of General Counsel	466,633	381,450
Data Systems / Development	381,710	1,390,500
Public Disclosure Division	1,102,782	1,713,550
Reports Analysis Division	345,497	293,778
Total	*30,175,983*	*36,850,000*

Source: *1998 FEC Annual Report*

Legislation

Data in Figure 7.2 indicates no correlation between legislation and enforcement. A review of the illustrative data appears to indicate that any change in enforcement over time is not systematically associated with the adoption of new legislation. There are a number of possible reasons for this finding. First, this might have to do with the magnitude and scope of the legislation itself. For example, following *Buckley v. Valeo* (1976) there have been only a handful of other pieces of legislation passed by Congress and signed by the president regarding FEC activity. Only the 1979 Amendments to the FECA abolishing FEC random audit power seems to have a significant influence on agency's enforcement actions. It is reasonable to expect that some legislation may not have a discernible correlation with FEC enforcement behavior until several years following its administrative implementation. Second, legislation indirectly influencing FEC organizational behavior may not be discernible by just examining the data over time. Indirect influence of legislation might be present in the case of the National Voter Registration Act of 1993 that assigned new administrative duties to the FEC. Due to this legislation, the agency's Office of Election Administration must research, inform, and monitor the implementation of the Act in support of state efforts to increase voter turnout. This piece of legislation forces FEC decision-makers to spread already thin administrative resources even thinner in efforts to implement the policy goals of the legislation. Third, any relationship might be non-linear and thus require additional statistical analysis that is beyond the scope of this research. In the end, the null hypothesis for legislative is accepted.

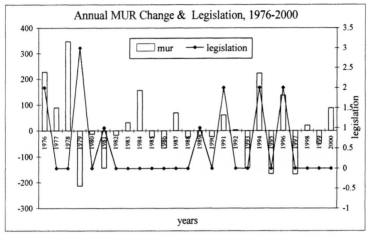

Figure 7.2.   MUR and Legislation, 1976-2000
Source: *Federal Election Commission Annual Reports* (1975-2000).

1998 FEC Legislation

While there is no single significant piece of legislation passed during 1998, in early 1999, the FEC did submit to the 105th Congress and the President two separate sets of legislative recommendations (1998 *FEC Annual Report*). The first set contained three recommendations that the Commission deem urgent. The second set of comments comprising 38 additional recommendations divided in two sections. The first section contained recommendations to ease the burden on political committees or to streamline administration of the law. The second section contained primarily technical recommendations aimed at correcting outdated or inconsistent parts of the law. The following will briefly address the Commissions *urgent recommendations*.

Urgent Recommendations

Electronic Filing Threshold. The Commission recommended that Congress give the FEC authority to require committees with a certain level of financial activity to file FEC reports electronically. The explanation for this recommendation is that Public Law 104-79 (1995) authorized electronic filing of disclosure reports with the FEC. As of 1997, political committees—except for Senate campaigns—may elect to file FEC reports electronically. The FEC has an electronic filing program and provides software to committees that will assist them in filing their reports electronically. To maximize the benefits of electronic filing, the Commission asked Congress to consider requiring committees that meet a certain threshold of financial activity to file their reports. Implementation of the recommendation would allow the FEC to receive, process, and disseminate the campaign finance data from electronically filed reports more efficiently, and thus, allow the agency to disseminate this information better. Adoption of this process should make committee filing duties and responsibilities easier to complete and enhance compliance with the law.

Campaign-Cycle Reporting Section. The Commission proposed that Congress revise the law and require authorized candidate committees to report on a campaign-to-date basis, rather than the traditional current calendar year basis. Presently, the Commission contends that authorized committees must track contributions received in two different ways. First, the committees must comply with the FECA reporting requirements that state committees must track donations on a calendar year basis. Second, for the committees to avoid violating various campaign contribution limits, they must track contributors' donations on a per-election basis. Simplifying FECA reporting requirements to allow reporting on a campaign-to-date rather than on a calendar year basis would reduce the burdensome nature of the law's record-keeping requirements. The Commission also recommended that contribution limits be determined on a campaign-cycle as well. A benefit of this proposed change, according to the Commission, is that it would enhance public disclosure of campaign finance activity. At that time individual itemization of contributions occurs only if the individual donates more than $200 (aggregate) during a calendar year. Itemization of disbursements occurs only if payments to a specific payee aggregate exceeding $200 during a calendar year. Itemization of contributions exceeding an aggregate of $200 for a single campaign-cycle captures public information that is currently not available.

Application of $25,000 Annual Limit. The Commission recommended that Congress modify the 1998 provision that limit individual contributions to $25,000 per calendar year so that an individual's contributions count against annual limits for the year in which the contribution is made. The law as of 1998 provided that a candidate contribution in a non-election year count against the individual donor's limit for the year in which the candidate's election takes place. This provision, according to the Commission, consistently confused many contributors. For example, a contributor wishing to support Candidate X in an election year contributes in the year before the election. The contributor reasonably assumes that the contribution counts against their limit for the year in which the contribution occurs. However, unaware that the contribution actually counts against the year in which Candidate X's election is held, the contributor makes other contributions during the election year, and thus, inadvertently might exceeds the then $25,000 limit. If requiring contributions to count against the limit of the calendar year in which the donor contributes, according to the Commission, the agency could reduce confusion and the number of inadvertent violations of the law. This enabled the Commission to better monitor annual contribution amounts (Table 7.5).

Table 7.5.   Selected Legislative Recommendations, 1998

Recommendation	Section
Urgent Recommendation	
Electronic Filing Threshold	2 U.S.C.&434(a)
Campaign-Cycle Reporting	2 U.S.C.&434
Application of $25,000 Annual Limit	2 U.S.C.&441a(a)(3)
Other Recommendations	
Incomplete or False Contributor Information	2 U.S.C.&434
Waiver Authority	2 U.S.C. &434
Point of Entry / Disclosure Documents	2 U.S.C.&434
Fraudulent Solicitation of Funds	2 U.S.C.&441h
Contributions by Foreign Nationals	2 U.S.C.&441e
Limitations for Contributions to Candidates	2 U.S.C.&441a
Distinguishing Campaign Travel	2 U.S.C.&431(9)
Contributions from Minors	2 U.S.C.&441a(a)(1)
Prohibition Against Reprisals	2 U.S.C.&441b(b)9(3)(A)
Fines for Reporting Violations	2 U.S.C.&437g
Criminal Provisions	2 U.S.C.&437g(a)(5)(C)&(d)
Audits for Cause	2 U.S.C.&438(b)
Modifying Terminology	2 U.S.C.&437g

Source: *1998 FEC Annual Report.*

Appointment

Data in Figure 7.3 appears to support Hypothesis 3 that there is a negative relationship between FEC appointments and enforcement. For example, during 1979, 1981 1985, 1986, 1998 when there are new Commissioners appointed to the FEC, we see significant downward trend in the annual number of new MUR cases. There are a number of reasons for this conclusion. First, appointment of new FEC Commissioners is primarily an exercise to balance political needs. New appointees may believe that partisan interests supporting their nomination and confirmation might expect the Commission to avoid imposing any additional costs upon their campaign or electoral efforts. New Commissioners may also realize that because there are numerous political and watchdog groups monitoring the agency's actions in relationship to their appointment, they may choose a conservative approach toward regulatory enforcement (Jackson 1990). Further, it may not be in the best interest of newly appointed Commissioners to engage in an activism enforcement agenda while serving on the Commission if they intend seek re-appointment (prior to 1998 FECA Amendments) or to some other politically sensitive position in government. Second, because FEC appointments primarily balance political interests, according the FECA, these appointees might lack the skill, training, and experience to perform their duties in an efficient and effective concerning the use of agency resources. Third, because there is a learning curve for new Commissioners, these appointees may slow enforcement activities. Anecdotal accounts contend that while senior Commissioners usually do not become more aggressive concerning enforcement matters during their latter years of service, political officials might become more uncertain about senor Commissioners' actions as these appointed officials might seek to institute agency policies that are not consistent with political desires. Thus, because the data presented in Figure 7.3 provides support for Hypothesis 3, rejection of the null hypothesis is appropriate. Nonetheless, due to regular political and campaign cycles, it is only prudent to be cautious when interpreting the data.

1998 FEC Appointments

The year 1998 begins for the FEC with a little reported but significant change to the FECA limits FEC Commissioners to serve only one six-year term. The Amendment at 2 U.S.C. $437c(a)(2)(A) strikes the phrase "for terms of 6 years" and adds in its place "for a single term of six years." The amendment is applicable to individuals nominated by the President after December 31, 1997, unless the President announced his intent to nominate an individual before November 30, 1997 (*The*

Record, January 1998). This change in the campaign finance law appeared to send a powerful message to incumbent Commissioners and potential members of the commission: you are politically responsible for your behavior while on the Commission. It is necessary to confess that while this statement of the proposed relationship between appointed Commissioners and hierarchical officials in government are only hypothetical, it is not beyond the bounds of reason. It is reasonable to expect that political officials would judge a Commissioner's service through a prism reflecting their own individual past, present, and future political interests. The following outlines the significant events and changes on the commission during 1998 as examples of how agency leadership influences the organization.

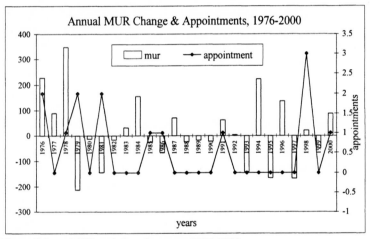

Figure 7.3.   MUR and Appointments, 1976-2000
Source: *Federal Election Commission Annual Reports* (1975-2000).

On August 11, 1998, Commissioner John Warren McGarry retired from the FEC after over 20 years of Commission service during four presidential administrations. McGarry was first appointed to the FEC in 1978 and re-appointed in 1983, 1989, and 1997. He last served as FEC Vice Chairman during 1996 and Chairman during 1997. McGarry's pivotal contributions to the agency's mission and programs, from full disclosure to uniform law enforcement, are testament to his public service. Colleagues report McGarry balanced fundamental First Amendment rights and government interests ensuring federal elections remain corruption free.

Chairman Joan Aikens also retired from the Commission after 23 years of Commission service. Chairman Aikens was President of the Pennsylvania Council of Republican Women and member of the Pennsylvania Republican State Committee was Appointed by President Ford and confirmed in 1975. Aikens was re-appointed in 1976, 1981, 1983, and 1989 by Presidents Reagan and Bush, having served four terms as Chairman (*The Record*, September 1998). Aikens is the longest serving member of the Commission in agency history, and due the recent imposition of term-limits, she will retain this distinction.

New Appointments

On July 30th, the Senate confirmed the re-nomination of Commissioner Scott Thomas and nominations of David Mason, Karl J. Sandstrom, and Daryl Wold. Vice Chairman Thomas initially was appointed to the Commission in 1986 by President Reagan and later re-appointed by President Bush in 1991. Thomas, a graduate of Stanford University and the Georgetown University Law Center served as assistant general counsel for enforcement, and assistant to former Commissioner Harris. There are three initial appointments. First, Mason is a former Senior Fellow at the Heritage Foundation, studying the research, writings, and commentary on Congress and national politics. Mason worked on Capital Hill for Senator John Warner, Representatives Tom Bliley and Trent Lott, and a deputy assistant secretary for the Department of Defense. He assumed the Commission seat vacant since Potter's 1995 resignation. Second, Sandstrom is a former chairman of the Department of Labor Administrative Review Board. Sandstrom, as a former Staff Director of the House Subcommittee on Elections, staff director of the House Task Force on Electoral Reform, deputy chief counsel to the House Administration Committee, and adjunct professor at American University, assumed the Commission seat vacated by McGarry. Third, Wold is a former private practice attorney in California specializing in business, election, and political law. He assumed the Commission seat previously occupied by Commissioner Aikens. Later in 2000, the Senate confirmed the nomination of Bradley A. Smith as a Commissioner on the FEC. Bradley is a former Professor of Law at Capital University Law School in Columbus, Ohio where he taught Election Law, Comparative Election Law, Jurisprudence, Law & Economics, and Civil Procedure.

Judicial

Data in Figure 7.4 does not point to a meaningful relationship between judicial decisions of the Supreme Court and FEC enforcement. Other then periods in 1994 and 1996, the empirical data does not provide systematic evidence that when the Court takes action concerning campaign finance related cases there is a positive correlation with FEC enforcement over time. There are a number of plausible reasons for this finding. First, although resolution of a campaign finance law case by the Supreme Court does reduce uncertainty, it cannot remove all agency doubt concerning future Court actions. Supreme Court consideration, review, and decisions are important as these actions dictate how the FEC should use resources related to the agency's commitment toward addressing long-term programmatic issues as opposed to short-term matters. Because the FEC has a long-term relationship with the Court and Justices, agency leadership may take special care to develop positive affiliations with judicial personnel. Agency response to Court actions, therefore, maybe predicated on its attempt to develop long-term strategies to facilitate favorable relationships as the prospect of frequent interactions with the judiciary and the possibility of institutional sanctions become more likely (Cover and Segal 1989; Epstein and George 1992). Second, not all cases the Supreme Court reviews concerning federal campaign finance law influence FEC administrative behavior equally. In the case of the *FEC v. NRA Political Victory Fund* (1994), the FEC had to halt all pending enforcement actions so that it could review past enforcement related decisions. While the assumption that FEC decision-makers respond symmetrically to all actions of the Supreme Court, this may not be the situation concerning all matters. Due to the unique nature of the agency's relationship with the Supreme Court, agency decision-makers probably use contextual, un-measurable information to respond appropriately to Court actions. This probably means that the relationship between Supreme Court action and FEC administrative behavior is perhaps so complex that identifying any significant correlation between the two variables is beyond the capabilities of this analysis. Thus, the null hypothesis is accepted.

1998 FEC Judicial Action

For the year 1998, there is one primary court case involving the FEC and the Supreme Court that shaped not only this relationship, but also the future administrative enforcement of campaign finance law. This case involved a test to the Commission's dismissal of an administrative complaint. In addition, there was another case involving a lawsuit filed after the Commission votes to take no action on an administrative complaint alleging campaign finance indiscretions regarding the executive office officials.

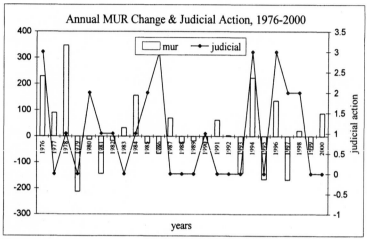

Figure 7.4.　　MUR and Judicial, 1976-2000.
Source:　　　*Federal Election Commission Annual Reports* (1975-2000).

FEC v. Akins, et al 96-1590

James Akins and associates filed an administrative complaint with the FEC alleging a lobbying group—the American Israel Public Affairs Committee (AIPAC)—failed to register and report as a political committee after making contributions to and expenditures on behalf of candidates in excess of $1,000. The FECA defined a political committee as any committee, relationship, or other group that receives contributions or makes expenditures to influence federal elections in excess of $1,000 during a calendar year (2 U.S.C. §431(4)(A)). However, a statutory exception to the definition of expenditure allows membership organizations to make disbursements of more than $1,000 for campaign-related communications to their members, without their counting as contributions or expenditures. AIPAC claims its communications to members fell within this exception and therefore did not have to register as a political committee or disclose its financial activities to the FEC. AIPAC contended disbursements qualify as expenditures because its members did not qualify as members under the Act. The FEC found AIPAC is not subject to the registration and disclosure rules applicable to political committees. The FEC believes because AIPAC major purpose is not influencing federal elections, it does not qualify as a political committee with expenditures exceeding $1,000 and dismisses the complaint.

Akins filed suit in U.S. District Court for the District of Columbia charging FEC failed to proceed on the administrative complaint and challenged the FEC interpretation of what constitutes a political committee. The District Court ruled in favor of the FEC that the "major purpose" tests that an organization receiving contributions or makes expenditures of more than $1,000 becomes a political committee only if its major purpose is the influencing of federal elections. Following this action, in 1995 the U.S. Court of Appeals for the District of Columbia rules FEC use of a "major purpose test" to narrow the definition of "political committee" is valid. Thus, its application of the "major purpose test" in this case was reasonable, and that its investigation into the matters rose by appellants was adequate. The court affirmed the district court's ruling dismissing appellants' complaint that FEC actions were contrary to law.

While the Court of Appeals affirmed the lower court ruling, an *en banc* panel of the same appellate court reversed the district court decision. The *en banc* panel found the major purpose test can only apply to organizations that make independent expenditures, not contributions, which is what was in question in the complaint against AIPAC. The Court also rejected the FEC argument that the appellants lack standing to bring their claim to federal court. On December 6, 1996, the U.S. Court of Appeals for the District of Columbia Circuit, sitting *en banc* reverses the district court's decision. On behalf of the FEC, the solicitor general appealed to the Supreme Court.

The Court also found that the plaintiffs' inability to obtain information about AIPAC campaign-related finances satisfied prudential standing. This is the kind of injury, according to the Court, the FECA does not address. The Court found the injury in this case was due to the fact that the plaintiffs were prevented from obtaining information about AIPAC donors and the organization's campaign-related contributions and expenditures, the injury is both "concrete" and "particular." The Court disagreed with the FEC position that the lawsuit involved only a "generalized grievance" shared by many. In such cases of "generalized grievance," the Court said the harm is usually "of an abstract and indefinite nature" not the kind of concrete harm that the court found here. The Court also found the harm asserted by the plaintiffs is traceable to the FEC decision to dismiss its administrative complaint, and that the courts have the power to redress this harm. The Supreme Court rejected the FEC argument that, because the agency's decision not to undertake an enforcement action is generally an area not subject to judicial review (2 U.S.C. §437g (a)(8)) its interpretation should be narrow. The Court referred the matter back to the FEC because of questions concerning the "membership" issue as applied to AIPAC (*The Record,* July 1998). On June 1, 1998, the U.S. Supreme Court ruled that Akins and other former government officials had standing to challenge in federal court the FEC dismissal of the 1989 administrative complaint against the AIPAC. The Supreme Court referred questions about membership back to the Commission.

Conclusion

This chapter provided an analysis of the relationship between FEC enforcement activity (i.e., administrative behavior) and elected official manipulation of agency resources (i.e., budget, legislation, appointment, and judicial action). By using a combination of qualitative and quantitative methodological research approaches, two kinds of information are gathered and analyzed to provide meaningful findings. In essence, case studies and longitudinal data used in this chapter present evidence that provide some support for the underlining assumption of this book is that due to the fundamental nature of campaign finance policy particular administrative arrangements are developed, and by extension, lead to certain administrative behavior by the FEC over time. Based on this analysis, independent variables that appear to have a significant relationship with FEC administrative behavior are agency budget and appointment of agency Commissioners. While these results cannot provide a comprehensive explanation regarding the entire range of political-administrative relationships, they do provide some insight into this matter.

Chapter VIII

Conclusion

There is a fundamental paradox concerning FEC administration and enforcement efforts to combat violations of campaign finance law and the agency's relationship to political officials. While campaign finance policy is similar to many other public policy areas in producing "winners" & "losers," unlike most other regulatory areas, the primary group of "winners" & "losers" regarding campaign finance policy are the same elected officials that create the 'rules of the game' that administer, implement, and enforce these regulation. This possible conflict of interest might have significant ramifications concerning if administration and enforcement of campaign finance law leads to outcomes that are consistent with the tenets of democracy. This book examined this issue through an analysis of the relationship between politically determined variables, (i.e., budget, legislation, appointment, and judicial action) and FEC administrative behavior over time. The following sections address the findings of the analysis conducted in this book, with special attention to the relevance of democratic theory to pubic policy and its significance to political-administrative studies.

Summary

This book provided a number of interesting general findings about the political-administrative relationship and specific finding about the FEC and its relationship with political officials. Chapter 1 highlighted the importance of democratic theory and the dynamic nature of policy-making in the context of a complex modern democratic society. This information helped to provide a context for a realistic assessment of how the public policy process works and the possibility of it producing policy outcomes that are consistent with democratic theory and government.

Chapter 2 focused on the importance of properly understanding electorate knowledge of political-related matters and why this information is important toward developing meaningful expectations about public involvement in the political and policy process. An important point noted in this chapter is that due to the complexity and scope of modern public policy, it is unrealistic to expect anyone other than full-time policy experts to understand and influence how policy is developed, administered, and enforced. Thus, public policy, for the most part, is determined by political and policy experts that create administrative arrangements that have a special interest bias that might increase the probability of producing undemocratic policy outcomes. In the case of the FEC and election policy, this might mean sub-optimal administration and enforcement of campaign finance law. This sub-optimal regulatory activity might allow some interests an unfair advantage in democratic elections through their ability to manipulate campaign finance law, and thus, avoid detection primarily due to inefficient and ineffective FEC administrative arrangements.

Chapter 3 documented the history of government efforts in the United States to regulate the use of money in politics from the late 1800s to the present, noting that over time the use of money in politics has become increasingly complex. While much of this information is currently available in the existing literature, its presentation in this book provided the historical context necessary to develop a meaningful appreciation for this policy issue. This information, in addition, illustrated the political context that lead to the establishment of the FEC and fundamental expectations regarding its administrative and structural development.

Chapter 4 used organization theory to develop an applied model for understanding the institutional-organizational relationship between the actions of the FEC and political official manipulation of critical agency resources. This theoretical model facilitated a comprehensive analysis of a complex institutional-organizational relationship and the development of testable hypotheses. Information presented in the chapter was valuable not only toward framing an analysis of the FEC specifically, but also the political-administrative relationship in general.

Chapter 5 provided a comprehensive overview of the FEC and its ability to administrate and enforce federal campaign finance law. There are two relevant points to make regarding this information. First, the analysis showed FEC staff must navigate through a changing web of administrative and enforcement procedures that are not only time consuming, but also place a heavy demand on agency resources. Second, because political officials over time have developed administrative arrangements for the FEC that allow multiple political interests access to FEC processing of enforcement matters, agency investigations of possible violations of the FECA is anything but effective or efficient. At times, these interventions on the part of political interests into FEC enforcement investigations have brought the agency to a virtual stand-still.

Chapter 6 highlighted relevant literature that outlines the debate between the administrative autonomy and political control perspectives concerning organizational behavior. This literature notes that political officials have at their disposal budgetary, legislative, appointment, and judicial tools—as shaped by agency administrative arrangements—that can be used to influence a regulatory agency's administrative behavior. Based on this literature review, agency data, and historical accounts, several testable hypotheses were developed. The appropriate method-ology for testing the hypotheses, in addition, was presented to provide scholarly rigor.

Chapter 7 featured results of case study analysis concerning the re-lationship between FEC enforcement of campaign finance law and the selected independent variables. This analysis looked at the possible relationship between changes in the annual number of new enforce-ment investigations opened by the FEC, known as MURs, and various politically determined organization-level independent variables (i.e., budget, legislative, appointment, and judicial) over a 25 year period and what, if any, role agency administrative arrangements play in these hypothesized relationships. The analysis concluded that while there might be a relationship between FEC administrative behavior and two of the four independent variables (i.e., budget and appointment), equally important is the acknowledgement that FEC administrative arrangements help to shape the scope and magnitude of agency actions. The data supported the assumptions that various administrative ar-rangements are important regarding political-administrative relation-ships. Table 8.1 summarizes these findings.

It is important to note that these specific findings regarding test-able hypotheses are intended to present only a limited representation of the broader, and more important, political-administrative relationship. Only by conducting this systematic analysis of the FEC and its rela-tionship to political institutions can we develop a meaningful assess-ment of democratic government.

Table 8.1.   Summary: FEC Administrative Behavior

Administrative Arrangements

- Structure (budget and appointments): The simple and centralized hierarchical formation of FEC organizational structure appears to facilitate political influence through the manipulation of institutional resources.

- Management (legislation and judicial): FEC bargaining enforcement style might disadvantage political grassroots organizations while possibly enhancing the fortunes of social and economic elite groups and interests.

Test Hypotheses

- Budget (*Positive Relationship*)
  There appears be to a positive relationship between FEC administrative behavior and FEC annual budget changes over time.
  [Finding: Null hypothesis *rejected*].

- Legislation (*Negative Relationship*)
  There does not appear to be a relationship between FEC administrative behavior and legislative enactment over time. The data does, however suggest that FEC administrative behavior relates more to the legislative processes itself than actual enacted legislation.
  [Finding: Null hypothesis *accepted*].

- Appointment (*Negative Relationship*)
  There appears to be a negative relationship between FEC administrative behavior and appointment of new FEC Commissioners over time.
  [Finding: Null hypothesis *rejected*].

- Judicial (*Positive Relationship*)
  This is a *prima facie* case for a positive relationship between FEC administrative behavior and Supreme Court action not supported by the evidence and analysis. An explanation for this finding might be that issue complexity and context of judicial matters simply do not produce quantifiable results.
  [Finding: Null hypothesis *accepted*].

Public Policy and Democratic Theory

Returning to a question presented earlier regarding which type of democratic theory and view of citizenship seems to provide the best explanation (i.e., policy-process model) of FEC administrative behavior over time? Based on complexity (e.g., financial and constitutional issues), scope (e.g., policy-makers and administration matters), and interest (e.g., ideological and political positions) relating to campaign finance policy, as a public policy it appears most consistent with a top-down policy process model. Due to the nature of the campaign finance regulation policy, a top-down policy process model seems to provide the best explanation for how policy ideas relating to campaign finance regulation move from informal discussion, onto the formal agenda, and finally to implementation.

If using a top-down policy-process model regarding public elections, campaign finance regulation appears most consistent with the consent view of citizenship and protective type of democracy. According to the consent view of citizenship, due to issues of policy complexity, scope, and interest, the general electorate has almost no choice but to abdicate majority responsibility of policy in this area to professional government officials and policy entrepreneurs. A primary reason for this is that the requirements necessary for public participation generate costs that over time are simply unsustainable for non-policy professionals to pay. For protective type of democracy, the historical record indicates that at best, the public's primary concern with money in campaigns and politics is the safeguarding of the integrity of federal elections. Most citizens do not advocate extensive change in campaign finance-related policy for either 'moral enlightenment' or 'self-determining' purposes. While the electorate may not have a sustained interest in campaign finance regulation, there is an identifiable segment of the society that has the time, skill, and resources to undertake such an activity: political officials and related elite policy entrepreneurs.

As noted earlier, political officials can choose to pay lax attention (i.e., fire-alarm oversight) or close attention (i.e., police-patrol oversight) to a specific policy issue. Because the issue of campaign finance regulation, and its enforcement, is of such great importance to individual and collective political interest, it is only reasonable that elected officials opt for police-patrol oversight. The selection of police-patrol oversight is not only consistent with elected officials' interests, but also with the issue of policy complexity and scope. Because campaign finance regulation constantly deals with issues addressing constitutional questions about property rights and freedom of speech, it is only appropriate that elected officials remain in a state of hyper-awareness of potential reform of election policy. Justification of political officials adopting a police-patrol oversight approach concerning campaign finance regulation is consistent with: (a) intense personal interests in maintaining elected office and (b) a possible deep belief in protecting of constitutional rights. To content that one justification is of greater importance to public officials than the other is simply unknowable.

There is an additional point concerning the design and use of enforcement models by the FEC. The deterrence enforcement model may tend to be more costly for the FEC while less costly for the regulated industry concerning resolution of disputed violations of the law. Under deterrence enforcement model, because the "rules of the game" are clear, there is greater responsibility on the FEC to (a) be very effective in each case and (b) efficiently move the enforcement process along. However, when using a conciliatory enforcement model instead of deterrence enforcement model, because the "rules of the game" are more open to interpretation, agency expectations are lower concerning enforcement effectiveness and efficiency. Thus, while the conciliatory enforcement model may tend to lower the cost of campaign finance regulation for political and industry stakeholders due to efficient enforcement, the bargaining enforcement model may tend to increase the cost of campaign finance regulation due to its relatively less efficient processes. This could mean that the bargaining enforcement model used by the FEC could disadvantage grassroots organizations from effectively advocating the FEC to pursue possible and specific violators of the FECA.

A review of FEC enforcement process, as discussed earlier, also provides interesting additional information on this matter. The FEC conciliatory enforcement model is structured around numerous checkpoints within the enforcement review process that allow politically appointed Commissioners the ability to administratively slow investigations or completely bring an investigation to a halt. In either case, because of flexible standards concerning what constitutes a "reason-to-believe" or a "no-reason-to-believe" finding, review of cases concerning possible violation of the FECA are open to the charge of being capricious. The conciliation enforcement model used by the FEC appears to place a greater resource responsibility on the filer of a report concerning a possible violation of the FECA than a deterrence enforcement model might. By its very nature, the conciliatory enforcement model prolongs investigations and allows time to elapse, while simultaneously draining resources from all those involved. Thus, the conciliatory enforcement model used by the FEC could favor the resource rich (e.g., business, labor, and professional political interests) and act as a disincentive for others (e.g., grassroots organizations) to report violations. This could reasonably be viewed as using a particular enforcement model in the context of a specific policy issue that enhances the probability of producing outcomes that are inconsistent with fundamental tenets of democratic theory and the promise of fair elections.

In the end, this book and its analysis provides two central lessons. First, that the special and unique features of individual public policies have significant influence on the type of administrative arrangements that are established and used to implement government public policy. Although this book provided a detailed examination of the complexity, scope, and interest of administrative behavior a specific policy—campaign finance and the FEC—this analysis is helpful when analyzing any number of other public policies and their administrative implementation. While campaign finance regulation has its own unique policy-related administrative issues, it nonetheless shares some similarities with other policy areas. One primary similarity is that conception, development, implementation, and review of a specific public policy occurs within certain political, social, institutional, and historical context that tend to have meaningful influence on policy administration and enforcement at every stage of its implementation. To discuss a public policy issue and related administrative arrangements without addressing important and relevant contextual factors could render a picture of the policy under analysis that might be theoretically profound, yet meaningless for all practical purposes.

Second, administrative arrangements matter regarding implementation of public policy that produces outcomes consistent with democratic theory and government. Since public policy is not self-executing, public officials must go about the arduous task of establishing specific rules and procedures that move public policy from abstract concept to tangible reality.

If the administrative arrangements developed for implementation of a public policy are too overbearing and result in the restriction of citizens' democratic rights, then the means may not justify the ends. Government administrative organizations are not in the business of efficiency solely; government administrative organizations are in the business of implementing promulgated public policy that seeks to resolve some identifiable social problem and enhance equality. This is not to say that public administrative agencies, like the FEC, are not concerned with operational efficiency, but only that operational effectiveness (i.e., meeting the democratically developed needs of citizens) should be their overarching goal. This book highlighted the need to remain focused on the fact that government organizations are part of the larger social-political and policy system. If we begin to lose sight of the democratic reasons for public administrative activities, we run the risk of becoming tangled in our own "rational chains."

Significance of Findings

The findings of this analysis are significant for two primary reasons. First is empirically highlighting the relationship between the complex nature of public policies and administrative arrangements that implement legislated remedies to identified collective action problems. The analysis underscores the diverse nature of public policy and their implementation in the United States. Policy-makers and government officials must develop appropriate policy and administration strategies that fall somewhere reasonably between theoretical and practical methodologies. When discussing what government should or should do regarding identified social problems, such as campaign finance regulation and the role of the FEC, we should avoid treating complex social issues similarly. Instead we need to realize the diverse nature of policies to develop appropriate administrative arrangements to implement policy solutions.

That said, structure and management arrangements are critical for effective and efficient implementation of public policy. Although implementation of policy is just one part of a broader policy process, nonetheless, this critical stage can determine the success or failure—however defined—of intended efforts to address identified collective problems. The key, as noted in this book, is that legislative creation of administrative agencies must carefully consider how administrative arrangements match with the particular policy issue the responsible government organization is addressing. Researchers and practitioners must note that partitioning of administrative agencies from their foundational public policy roots might lead to incomplete and inaccurate assessment of political-administrative relationships in the context of democratic government.

A second reason why this analysis is significant has to do with emphasizing the normative value of administrative arrangements and their importance regarding implementation of policy consistent with democratic theory and government. The analysis underscores that while objective estimates of administrative efficiency and effectiveness are necessary toward the procedural execution of politically developed policy as the produce of open and fair public elections, there is a deeper importance. Public consent of government policies provide administrative agencies their legitimacy to undertake an entire range of activities including tax collection, spending policies, wealth redistribution, and the prioritization of collective action through formal institutions. In this sense, the question of legitimacy is limited to those conventions that govern the relationship of citizens to the state, and securing that legitimacy through the consent of citizens. While there may be disagreement within government regarding the means appropriate to achieve these ends, this is nonetheless an indispensable part of modern democratic government. Thus, regardless of the particular model of policy-making used (bottom-up or top-down), public policy that is in accordance with fair elections and adheres to the tenets of democratic theory and government can be called legitimate by most. Is this traditional notion of government legitimacy concerning policy development and implementation in the United States adequate to maintain effective government?

Another view of government legitimacy concerning policy development and its implementation contends that in contemporary society questions concerning legitimacy arise in a much broader social context. That historical social practices, norms, and standards previously thought to constitute traditional notions of legitimate and illegitimate government action are more correctly viewed as conventions shaped by limited and narrow social politics. This means that to the extent historical policy action conflicts with the contemporary views, these might appear as odious constraints rather than enhancing individual freedom. Accordingly, determination of government legitimacy, and thus government actions, reaches beyond a "night-watchman" view of the state. Government legitimacy, according to this critical view, rests on the public sector's ability to adjust historically determined policies in a manner that more closely reflects the "will" of citizens through open, democratic processes. Issues of social concern previously viewed as being outside justifiable areas of vigorous government action, now become legitimate government action. Consequently, government failure this might constitute an illegitimate action (Habermas 1973).

Irrespective of the view of government legitimacy, the point is that as the nature and methods of conducting campaigns and elections in the United States evolves as part of a general modernization process, we may need to seriously re-examine traditional notions of democratic theory and government in order to establish new administrative standards that enhance government legitimacy. Regardless of either a traditional or a critical theory of government legitimacy, the point remains that democratic government must develop and implement policies that protect individual freedom and equality within democratic society.

In the end, this book emphasized the tenuous nature of insuring that public institutions and organizations provide the greatest opportunity for producing policy outcomes consistent with democratic theory and government by analyzing the FEC. Often politicians, special interests, and academics tend to become overly involved in the details of debating policy processes and procedures that leaves unanswered questions concerning the democratic nature of policy and its implementation. This statement is not casting blame on those involved in the development and implementation of public policy. Due to the fierce competition over scarce resources at all levels of society, some might take the position that it is only reasonable that greater attention focuses on policy means than ends. That said, however, all involved in the policy-making process are responsible for developing and implementing government solutions to societal problems that consider the democratic nature of public policy, to include policy development and its implementation. Thus the contribution this book makes to the analysis of public policy and public administration is to put policy and administrative studies in their proper place by refocusing attention on the democratic nature of government administrative action. This book is just one part of an ongoing process to protect democratic values and enhance administrative performance without diminishing individual liberty and human dignity.

Final Comments
This analysis highlighted the important relationships between politics, policy-making, administrative implementation, and democratic outcomes. By providing general and specific findings, this book enhances our understanding of how policy-type frames administrative arrangements policy outcome consistent with democratic theory. Specifically, this analysis revealed how political officials and government develop the creation of administrative arrangements is associated with FEC enforcement of campaign finance law in such a manner that might produce undemocratic policy outcomes. Thus, the administrative behavior of the FEC, and similar public agencies, depends not only on the level of resource support the agency receives from political institutions, but equally on the administrative design features policy-makers impose on the organization. Until the administration of campaign finance regulatory administration is elevated to the same level of importance as policy discussions concerning campaign finance law, effective enforcement will continue to be suspect in the eyes of the public. Equally important is the possible disenfranchisement of certain segments of society from participating in open and free federal elections. Hence, expanding our knowledge about the possible administrative consequences that may arise due to the actions of government officials

should make political and administrative decision-makers more accountable for the actions of public agencies in a democracy.

Bibliography

Adamany, D. (1972). *Campaign Finance in America.* North Scituate: Buxbury Press.

Adamany, D., & Agree, G. (1975). "Election Campaign Financing". *Political Science Quarterly, 90,* 202-211.

Akins v. FEC, 118 S. Ct. 1777 (1998).

Aldrich, J. (1995). *Why Parties?* Chicago: University of Chicago Press.

Alexander, H. (1971). *Financing the 1968 Election.* Lexington: Heath and Co.

Alexander, H. (1972). *Money In Politics.* Washington, DC: Public Affairs Press.

Alexander, H. (1976). *Financing the 1972 Election.* Washington, DC: Heath and Co.

Alexander, H. (1980). *Financing Politics* (3rd ed.). Washington, DC: Congressional Quarterly Press.

Alexander, H., & Bauer, M. (1991). *Financing the 1988 Election.* Boulder: Westview Press.

Allen, D., & Jensen, R. (Eds.). (1995). *Freeing the First Amendment.* New York: New York University Press.

Allison, G. (1971). *Essence of Decision.* Boston: Little, Brown.

Appleby, P. (1949). *Policy and Administration.* Alabama: University of Alabama Press.

Arneson, R. (1982). "The Principle of Fairness and Free-Rider Problems." *Ethics, 92,* 616-633.

Arrow, K. (1974). *The Limits of Organizations.* New York: Norton.

Athens Lumber Company v. FEC, 465 U.S. 1092 (1984).

Austin v. Michigan State Chamber of Commerce, 494 U.S. 652 (1990).

Austin-Smith, D. (1993). "Information and Influence." *American Journal of Political Science, 37,* 799-833.

Banks, J., & Weingast, B. (1992). "The Political Control of Bureaucracies Under Asymmetric Information." *American Journal of Political Science, 36,* 509-524.

Bachrach, P. (1980). *The Theory of Democratic Elitism: A Critique.* New York: University Press of America.

Barker, R. (1990). *Political Legitimacy and the State.* Oxford: Clarendon Press.

Barnard, C. (1938). *The Functions of the Executive.* Cambridge: Harvard University Press.

Barnum D. (1985). "The Supreme Court and Public Opinion: Judicial Decision-Making in the Post New Deal Period." *The Journal of Politics, 47,* 652-665.

Bates, R., & Bianco, W. (1990). "Cooperation by Design: Leadership, Structure, and Collective Dilemmas." *American Political Science Review, 84,* 133-147.

Bauer, R., & Kafka, D. (1984). *United States Federal Election Law.* Seattle: Oceana Publications.

Bawn, K. (1995). "Political Control Versus Expertise." *American Political Science Review, 89,* 62-73.

Bell, R. (1985). "Professional Values and Organizational Decision-Making." *Administration and Society, 17,* 21-60.

Bendor, J., & Moe, T. (1985). "An Adaptive Model of Bureaucratic Politics." *American Political Science Review, 79,* 755-774.

Bendor, J., & Mookherjee, D. (1987). "Institutional Structure and the Logic of Ongoing Collective Action." *American Political Science Review, 81,* 129-154.

Benson, G. (1978). *Political Corruption in America.* Lexington: Lexington Books.

Berry, J., & Goldman, J. (1973). "Congress and Public Policy." *Harvard Journal on Legislation, 10,* 331-365.

Blau, P. (1974). *On the Nature of Organizations.* New York: John Wiley.

Blau, P., & Schoenherr, R. (1971). *The Structure of Organizations.* New York: Basic Books.

Bozeman, B., Reed, P., & Scott, P. (1992). "The Presence and Predictability of Red Tape in Public and Private Organizations." *Administration and Society, 24,* 290-322.

Bread PAC v. FEC, 455 U.S. 577 (1984).

Brown, C., Powell, L., & Wilcox, C. (1995). *Serious Money.* Cambridge: Cambridge University Press.

Brumback, G. (1991). "Institutionalizing Ethics in Government." *Public Personnel Management, 20,* 353-364.

Buchanan, J., Tollison, R., & Tullock, G. (1980). *Toward a Theory of the Rent-Seeking.* College Station: Texas A&M University Press.

Buckley v. Valeo, 425 U.S. 946 (1976).

Bureau of Labor Statistics. [2000] *labstat.helpdesk@bls.gov*

Calvert, R., McCubbins, M., & Weingast, B. (1989). "A Theory of Political Control of Agency Discretion." *American Journal of Political Science, 33,* 588-610.

Campbell, A., Miller, W., & Converse, P. (1980). *American Voter.* Chicago: University of Chicago Press.

Canon, B., & Johnson, C. (1984). *Judicial Policies.* Washington, DC: Congressional Quarterly Press.

Carpenter, D. (1996). "Adaptive Signal Processing, Hierarchy, and Budgetary Control in Federal Regulation." *American Political Science Review, 90,* 283-302.

Christiano, T. (1996). *The Rule of the Many: Fundamental Issues in Democratic Theory.* Boulder: Westview Press.

Clifton v. FEC, 118 S. Ct. 1036 (1998).

Common Cause v. Schmitt, 455 U.S. 129 (1982).

Comptroller General of the United States. (1975). *Report of the Office of Federal Elections of the General Accounting Office in Administering the Federal Election Campaign Act of 1971.* Washington, DC: U.S. Government Printing Office.

Congressional Quarterly. (1982). *Dollar Politics* (3rd ed.). Washington, DC: Congressional Quarterly Press.

Conlon, R. (1987). "The Declining Role of Individual Contributions in Financing Congressional Campaigns." *Journal of Law and Politics, 3,* 467-498.

Corder, J. (1998). "The Politics of Federal Credit Subsidy." *American Review of Public Administration, 28,* 166-186.

Corrado, A., Mann, T., Ortiz, D., Potter, T., & Sorauf, F. (1997). *Campaign Finance Reform.* Washington, DC: Brookings Institution.

Cover, A., & Segal, J. (1989). "Ideological Values and the Votes of Supreme Court Justices." *American Political Science Review, 83,* 557-565.

Crozier, M. (1964). *The Bureaucratic Phenomenon.* London: Tavistock.

Cyert, R., & March, J. (1963). *A Behavioral Theory of the Firm.* Englewood Cliffs: Prentice-Hall.

Danziger, S., & Gottschalk, P. (1995). *America Unequal.* Cambridge: Harvard University Press.

Delli Carpini, M., & Keeter, S. (1991). *What Americans Know about Politics and Why It Matters.* New Haven: Yale University Press.

Democratic Senatorial Campaign Committee v. FEC, 454 U.S. 27 (1981).

Denhardt, R. (1992). "Morality as an Organizational Problem." *Public Administration Review, 52*, 104-105.

Desveaux, J. (1995). *Designing Bureaucracies.* Stanford: Stanford University Press.

Diamond, M. (1993). *The Unconscious Life of Organizations.* Westport: Quorum Books.

Dodd, L., & Schott, R. (1986). *Congress and the Administrative State* (2nd ed.). New York: MacMillian.

Donaldson, L. (1996). *For Positivist Organization Theory.* Thousand Oaks: Sage Publications.

Downs, A. (1957). *An Economic Theory of Democracy.* New York: Harper and Row.

Downs, A. (1967). *A Theory of Bureaucracy.* Boston: Little, Brown.

Drew, E. (1983). *Politics and Money.* New York: MacMillian.

Dye, T. 2002. *Understanding Public Policy.* (10th ed.). New Jersey: Prentice Hall.

Eavery, C., & Miller, G. (1984). "Bureaucratic Agenda Control." *American Political Science Review, 78*, 719-733.

Edelman, M. (1971). *Politics as Symbolic Action.* Chicago: Markham Publishing.

Eisner, M., & Meier, K. (1990). "Presidential Control Versus Bureaucratic Power." *American Journal of Political Science, 34*, 269-87.

Epstein, L., & George, T. (1992). "On the Nature of Supreme Court Decision-Making." *American Political Science Review, 86*, 323-337.

Ethics Reform Act Amendments of 1989, Pub. L. No. 101-194 (1989).

Etzioni, A. (1984). *Capital Corruption.* New York: Harcourt, Brace, Jovanovich.

Federal Election Campaign Act of 1971, Pub. L. No. 92-225 (1971).

Federal Election Campaign Act Amendments of 1974, Pub. L. No. 93-443 (1994).

Federal Election Campaign Act Amendments of 1976, Pub. L. No. 94-283 (1976).

Federal Election Campaign Act Amendments of 1979, Pub. L. No. 96-187 (1979).

FEC v. Colorado Republican Federal Campaign Committee, 116 S. Ct. 2309 (1996).

FEC v. Massachusetts Citizens for Life, 479 U.S. 238 (1986).

FEC v. National Conservative Political Action Committee, 470 U.S. 480 (1985).

126   The Federal Election Commission

FEC v. National Rifle Relationship Political Victory Fund, 513 U.S. 88
    (1993).
FEC v. National Right to Work Committee, 459 U.S. 197 (1982).
FEC v. Political Contributions Data, 943 F2d 190 (2d Cir 1991)
    (1991).
FEC v. Williams, 118 S. Ct. 52 (1997).
Federal Corrupt Practices Act, 43 U.S.C Stat. 1070 (1925).
Federal Election Commission. (1975-2000). *Annual Report of the Fed-
    eral Election Commission.* Washington, DC: U.S. Government
    Printing Office.
Federal Election Commission. (1994). *Federal Election Commission:
    Twenty-Year Report, April 1995.* Washington, DC: U.S. Gov-
    ernment Printing Office.
Federal Election Commission. (2000). *FEC Reports Increase In Party
    Fundraising For 2000* [Online]. Available:
    http://www.fec.gov/press/press2001/051501partyfund.html.
    [2001, December 5].
Federal Election Commission. (1999). *Selected Court Case Abstract,
    1976-1999* (16th ed.). Washington, DC: U.S. Government Print-
    ing Office.
Fenno, R. (1966). *The Power of the Purse.* Boston: Little, Brown.
Ferejohn, J., & Shipan, C. (1990). "Congressional Influence on Bu-
    reaucracy." *Journal of Law, Economics and Organization, 6,* 1-
    20.
Ferguson, T. (1995). *Golden Rule.* Chicago: University of Chicago
    Press.
Finocchiaro, M. (1999). *Beyond Right and Left: Democratic Elitism in
    Mosca and Gramsci.* New Haven: Yale University Press.
Fiorina, M. (1979). *Control of Bureaucracy.* St. Louis: Center for the
    Study of American Business.
Fiorina, M. (1982). "Legislative Choice of Regulatory Reforms." *Pub-
    lic Choice, 39,* 33-66.
First National Bank of Boston V. Bellotti, 435 U.S. 765 (1978).
Fisher, L. (1993). *The Politics of Shared Power* (3rd ed.). Washington,
    DC: Congressional Quarterly Press.
Gais, T. (1996). *Improper Influence.* Ann Arbor: University of Michi-
    gan Press.
General Accounting Office. *Independent Counsel: Expenditure and
    Other Information for the Office of Independent Counsel Ken-
    neth W. Starr/Robert W. Ray.* AIMD-00-283R August 22,
    2000.

Gerber, B., & Teske, P. (2000). "Regulatory Policymaking in the American States: A Review of Theories and Evidence." *Political Research Quarterly, 53,* 849-886.

Glantz, S., Abramowitz, A., & Burkart, M. (1976). "Election Outcomes." *The Journal of Politics, 34,* 1033-1038.

Goodin, R. (1996). *The Theory of Institutional Design.* Cambridge: Cambridge University Press.

Goodnow, F. (1900). *Policy and Administration.* New York: Macmillan.

Gormley, W. (1998). "Regulatory Enforcement Styles." *Political Research Quarterly, 51,* 363-383.

Gross, K. (1991). "The Enforcement of Campaign Finance Rules." *Yale Law and Policy Review, 9,* 279-300.

Gross, K., & Hong, K. (1998). "The Criminal and Civil Enforcement of Campaign Finance Laws." *Stanford Law and Policy Review, 10,* 51-64.

Gunlicks, A.. (1993). (Ed.). *Campaign and Party Finance in North America and Western Europe.* Boulder: Westview Press.

Habermas, J. (1973). *Legitimation Crisis.* Boston: Bacon.

Habermas, J. (1990). *Moral Consciousness and Communicative Action.* Cambridge: MIT Press.

Hall, R., & Quinn, R. (Eds.). (1983). *Organizational Theory and Public Policy.* Beverly Hills: Sage.

Hall, R., & Wayman, F. (1990). "Buying Time." *American Political Science Review, 84,* 797-820.

Hamilton, J. (Ed.). (1994). "Regulating Regulation." *Law and Contemporary Problems, 57,* 1-185.

Hamman, J. (1993). "Bureaucratic Accommodation of Congress and the President." *Political Research Quarterly, 46,* 863-879.

Hatch Act, 54 U.S.C. Stat. 767 (1940).

Hatch, M. (1997). *Organization Theory.* New York: Oxford University Press.

Heap, S., Hollis, M., Lyons, B., Sugden, R., & Weale, A. (1992). *The Theory of Choice.* Cambridge: Basil Blackwell.

Heidenheimer, A. (1970). *Political Corruption.* New York: Holt, Rinehart, and Winston.

Hibbing, J., & Welch, S. (1997). "The Effects of Charges of Corruption on Voting Behavior in Congressional Elections, 1982-1990." *The Journal of Politics, 59,* 226-239.

Hickson, D., Hinings, C., Lee, C., Schneck, R., & Pennings, J. (1971). "A Strategic Contingencies Theory of Intra-Organizational Power." *Administrative Science Quarterly, 16,* 216-229.

Hoerrner, K. (1999). "Symbolic Politics." *Journalism and Mass Communication Quarterly, 76,* 684-698.

Hoffman, T. (1998). "Rationality Reconceived." *Critical Review, 12,* 459-480.

Holden, B. (1988). *Understanding Liberal Democracy.* Oxford: Phillip Allen.

Horn, M. (1995). *The Political Economy of Public Administration.* Cambridge: Cambridge University Press.

House Point-of-Entry Act of 1996, Pub. L. No. 104-79 (1996).

Jackson, B. (1990). *Broken Promise.* New York: Priority Press Publication.

Jacobson, G. (1980). *Money in Congressional Elections.* New Haven: Yale University Press.

James, S. (1996). "The Political and Administrative Consequences of Judicial Review." *Public Administration, 74,* 613-637.

Jenkins-Smith, H., & Sabatier, P. (1993). *Policy Change and Learning.* Boulder: Westview Press.

Johnson, C. (1979). Judicial Decisions and Organizational Change. *Law and Society Review, 14,* 27-56.

Johnson, C. (1992). *The Dynamics of Conflict Between Bureaucrats and Legislators.* Armonk: M.E. Sharpe.

Katz, R. (1994). "Electoral Policy." In S. Nagel (Ed.), *Encyclopedia of Policy Studies* (2nd ed.) (329-354). New York: Marcel Dekker, Inc.

Katzmann, R. (1980). "Judicial Intervention and Organization Theory." *The Yale Law Journal, 89,* 513-537.

Kaufman, H. (1973). *Administrative Feedback: Monitoring Subordinates' Behavior.* Washington, DC: The Brookings Institution.

Kaufman, H. (1976). *Are Governmental Organizations Immortal?* Washington, DC: The Brookings Institute.

Kaufman, H. (1981). *The Administrative Behavior of Federal Bureau Chiefs.* Washington, DC: The Brookings Institution.

Kiewiet, D., & McCubbins, M. (1988). "Presidential Influence on Congressional Appropriations." *American Journal of Political Science, 32,* 714-736.

Kiewiet, D., & McCubbins, M. (1991). *The Logic of Delegation.* Chicago: University of Chicago Press.

King, G., Keohane, R., and Verba, S. (1994). *Designing Social Inquiry: Scientific Inference in Qualitative Research.* Princeton: Princeton University Press.

Kingdon, J. (1984). *Agenda, Alternatives, and Public Politics.* Boston: Little, Brown.

Knight, R. (1962). *Silent Spring*. Boston: Houghton Mifflin.

Koven, S. (1994). "The Bureaucracy-Democracy Conundrum: A Contemporary Inquiry into the Labyrinth." In A. Farazmand (Ed.), *Handbook of Bureaucracy*. New York: Marcel Dekker, Inc.

Krause, G. (1996). "The Institutional Dynamics of Policy Administration." *American Journal of Political Science, 40*, 1083-1121.

Krebhbiel, K. (1991). *Information and Legislative Organization*. Ann Arbor: University of Michigan Press.

Lebovic, J. (1995). "How Organizations Learn." *American Journal of Political Science, 39*, 835-863.

Leibenstein, H. (1987). *Inside the Firm*. Cambridge: Harvard University Press.

Light, P. (1995). *Thickening Government*. Washington, DC: Brookings Institution.

Macey, J. (1992). "Organizational Design and Political Control of Administrative Agencies." *The Journal of Law, Economics, & Organization, 8*, 93-110.

Magleby, D., & Holt, M. (1999). "Soft Money and Issue Advocacy." *Campaigns & Elections, 20*, 22-27.

Maine Right to Life v. FEC. (1997). 118 S. Ct. 52.

Mainzer, L. (1973). *Political Bureaucracy*. Glenview: Scott-Foresman.

Malbin, M. (Ed.). (1984). *Money and Politics in the United States*. Chatham: Chatham House Publishers.

March, J. (1997). "Administrative Practice, Organization Theory, and Political Philosophy: Ruminations on the Reflections of John M. Gaus." *PS: Political Science and Politics, 30*, 689-698.

March, J., & Olsen, J. (1989). *Rediscovering Institutions*. New York: Free Press.

March, J., & Simon, H. (1958). *Organizations*. New York: John Wiley.

Marshaw, J. (1994). "Improving the Environment of Agency Rulemaking: An Essay on Management, Games, and Accountability." *Law and Contemporary Problems, 57*, 185-257.

Marx, K. (1977). *Karl Marx: Selected Writings*. D. McLellan (Ed.). Oxford: Oxford University Press.

Matthews, D. (1994). *Politics for People*. Chicago: University of Illinois.

Mayhew, D. (1974). *Congress*. New Haven: Yale University Press.

Mayhew, D. (1991). *Divided We Govern*. New Haven: Yale University Press.

Mazmanian, D., & Sabatier, P. (1989). *Implementation and Public Policy*. Lantham: University Press of America.

McCarthy, M. (1972). *Elections For Sale*. Boston: Houghton Mifflin.

McCubbins, M., Noll, R., & Weingast, B. (1989). "Structure and Process as Solutions to the Politicians Principal-Agency Problem." *Virginia Law Review, 74,* 431-482.

McCubbins, M., Noll, R., & Weingast, B. (1990). "Administrative Procedures as Instruments of Political Control." *Journal of Law, Economics and Organization, 3,* 243-277.

McCubbins, M. & Schwartz, T. (1984). "Congressional Oversight Overlooked: Police Patrols versus Fire Alarms." *American Journal of Political Science, 28,* 165-179.

McFarland, A. (1984). *Common Cause.* Chatham: Chatham House Publishers.

McLean, I. (1991). "Rational Choice and Politics." *Political Studies, 39,* 496-512.

Meier, K. (1987). *Politics and the Bureaucracy.* Monterey: Brooks and Cole.

Melnick, R. (1983). *Regulation and the Courts.* Washington, DC: Brookings Institution.

Miller, D. (1991). *The Blackwell Encyclopedia of Political Thought.* Cambridge: Basil Blackwell.

Moe, T. (1982). "Regulatory Performance and Presidential Administration." *American Journal of Political Science, 26,* 197-224.

Moe, T. (1984). "The New Economics of Organization." *American Journal of Political Science, 28,* 739-777.

Moe, T. (1995). "The Politics of Structural Choice: Toward a Theory of Public Bureaucracy." In O Williamson (Ed.), *Organization Theory: From Chester Barnard to the Present and Beyond.* New York: Oxford University Press.

Moe, T., & Wilson, S. (1994). "Presidents and the Politics of Structure." *Law and Contemporary Problems, 57,* 1-44.

Morrow, J. (1994). *Game Theory for Political Scientists.* Princeton: Princeton University Press.

Morton, R. (1999). *Methods and Models.* Cambridge: Cambridge University Press.

Mosher, F. (Ed.). (1976). *Basic Documents of American Public Administration, 1776-1950.* New York: Holmes and Meier.

National Chamber Alliance Politics v. FEC, 445 U.S. 954 (1980).

National Voter Registration Act of 1994, Pub. L. No. 103-31 (1993).

Newberry v. United States, 256 U.S. 232 (1921).

Niskanen, W. (1971). *Bureaucracy and Representative Government.* Chicago: Aldine-Atherton.

Niskanen, W. (1994). *Bureaucracy and Public Economics.* Brookfield: Edward Elgar.

North, D. (1990). *Institutions, Institutional Change and Economic Performance.* Cambridge: Cambridge University Press.

Oldaker, W. (1986). "Of Philosophers, Foxes, and Finances: Can the Federal Election Commission Ever Do an Adequate Job*?*" *The Annals of the American Academy, 486,* 132-145.

Olson, M. (1982). *The Rise and Decline of Nations.* New Haven: Yale University Press.

Omnibus Budget Reconciliation Act of 1993, Pub. L. No. 103-66, (1993).

Ostrom, E. (1991). "Rational Choice Theory and Institutional Analysis: Toward Complementarity." *American Political Science Review, 85,* 237-243.

Overacker, L. (1932). *Money in Elections.* New York: Macmillan.

Page, E. (1985). *Political Authority and Bureaucratic Power.* Brighton: Harvester Press.

Parsons, T. (1956). "Suggestions for a Sociological Approach to the Theory of Organizations." *Administrative Science Quarterly, 1,* 63-85.

Pateman, C. (1970). *Participation and Democratic Theory.* Cambridge: Cambridge University Press.

Peabody, R., & Berry, J. (1972). *To Enact A Law.* New York: Praeger.

Peltzman, S. (1976). "Toward a More General Theory of Regulation." *Journal of Law and Economics, 19,* 211-40.

Pendleton Act, 22 U.S.C. Stat. 2 (1883).

Peters, B. (1984). *The Politics of Bureaucracy.* New York: Longman.

Peters, B., & Savoie, D. (1996). Managing Incoherence. *Public Administration Review, 56,* 281-290.

Pfeffer, J. (1982). *Organizations and Organization Theory.* Marshfield: Pitman Press.

Pfeffer, J. (1997). *New Directions for Organization Theory.* New York: Oxford University Press.

Pfeffer, J., & Salancik, G. (1978). *The External Control of Organizations.* New York: Harper and Row.

Potter, T., & McDonald, D. (1994). *FEC Letter to Robert Livingston, Subcommittee on Elections, Committee on House Administration* (dtd: July 19,1994).

Pricewaterhouse Coopers. (1999). *Technology and Performance Audit and Management Review of the Federal Election Commission: Final Report.* New York: Author.

Publicity Act, 36 U.S.C. Stat. 822 (1910).

The Record. (May 1998). Volume 24, Number 5. Federal Election Commission.

The Record. (January 1998). Volume 24, Number 1. Federal Election Commission.

Renstrom, P. (1991). *The American Law Dictionary.* Santa Barbara: ABC-Clio.

Renstrom, P., & Rogers, C. (1989). *The Electoral Politics Dictionary.* Santa Barbara: ABC-Clio.

Reorganization Plan No. 2 of 1973, Pub. L. No. 93-253 (1981).

Republican National Committee v. FEC, 445 U.S. 955 (1980).

Ringquist, E. (1995). Political Control and Policy Impact in EPA's Office of Water Quality. *American Journal of Political Science, 39,* 336-363.

Ripley, R. (1967). *Party Leaders in the House of Representatives.* Washington, D.C.: Brookings Institute.

Ripley, R. (1986). *Policy Implementation and Bureaucracy* (2nd ed.). Chicago: Dorsey Press.

Ripley, R., & Franklin, G. (1991). *Congress, the Bureaucracy and Public Policy* (5th ed.). Homewood: Dorsey.

Sabatier, P., & Mazmanian, D. (1979). "The Conditions of Effective Implementation." *Policy Analysis, 5,* 481-504.

Sabato, L. (1984). *PAC Power: Inside the World of Political Action Committees.* New York: W.W. Norton.

Sabato, L. (1989). *Paying for Elections.* New York: Priority Press.

Sabato, L., & Simpson, G. (1996). *Dirty Little Secrets.* New York: Random House.

Samples, J., Palmer, T., & Basham, P. (2001). *Lessons of Election 2000.* Washington, DC: CATO Institute.

Sandel, M. (1996). *Democracy's Discontent: America In Search of a Public Philosophy.* Cambridge: Harvard University Press.

Scholz, J. (1991). "Cooperative Regulatory Enforcement and The Politics of Administrative Effectiveness." *American Political Science Review, 85,* 115-136.

Scholz, J., & Pinney, N. (1995). "Duty, Fear, and Tax Compliance." *American Journal of Political Science, 39,* 490-512.

Scholz, J., & Wei, F. (1986). "Regulatory Enforcement in a Federalist System." *American Political Science Review, 79,* 1249-1270.

Scott, P. (1997). "Assessing Determinants of Bureaucratic Discretion: An Experiment in Street-Level Decision Making." *Journal of Public Administration Research and Theory, 7,* 35-57.

Scott, R. (1975). "Organizational Structure." *Annual Review of Sociology, 1,* 1-25.

Shapiro, M. (1968). *The Supreme Court and Administrative Agencies.* New York: Free Press.

Simon, H. (1957). *Administrative Behavior* (2nd ed.). New York: Free Press.

Smith, A. (1978). *Adam Smith and the Wealth of Nations.* F. Glahe (Ed.). Boulder: Colorado Associated University Press.

Smith, C. (1993). *Courts and the Public Policy.* Chicago: Nelson-Hall Publishers.

Smolla, R. (1992). *Free Speech in an Open Society.* New York: Alfred Knopf.

Sorauf, F. (1992). *Inside Campaign Finance.* New York: Yale University Press.

Spriggs, J. (1996). "The Supreme Court and Federal Administrative Agencies." *American Journal of Political Science, 40,* 1122-1151.

Stern, R., & Barley, S. (1997). "Organizations and Social Systems." *Administrative Science Quarterly, 41,* 146-162.

Stigler, G. (1971). "The Theory of Economic Regulation." *Bell Journal of Economics, 2,* 3-21.

Taft-Hartley Act, 61 U.S.C. Stat. 136 (1947).

Terry, L. (1990). Leadership in the Administrative State. *Administration and Society, 21,* 395-413.

Terry, L. (1995). *Leadership of Public Bureaucracies.* Thousand Oaks: Sage.

Teske, P. (1991). "Interests and Institutions in State Regulation." *American Journal of Political Science, 35,* 139-154.

Thayer, G. (1973). *Who Shakes the Money Tree?* New York: Simon and Schuster.

Tillman Act, 34 U.S.C. Stat. 864 (1907).

Tufte, E. (1983). *The Visual Display of Quantitative Information.* Cheshire: Graphics Press.

Truman, D. (1959). *The Congressional Party.* New York: John Wiley.

Tullock, G. (1965). *The Politics of Bureaucracy.* Washington, DC: Public Affairs Press.

Tullock, G. (1989). *The Economics of Special Privilege and Rent Seeking.* Boston: Kluwer Academic Publishers.

United States v. Classic. 314 U.S. 707 (1941).

Von Neumann, J & Morgenstern, O. (1944). *Theory of Games and Economic Behavior.* Princeton: Princeton University Press.

Waldo, D. (1948). *The Administrative State* (2nd ed.). New York: Holmes and Meier.

Waldo, D. (1978). "Organization Theory." *Public Administration Review, 38,* 589-597.

Webb, E., & Weick, K. (1979). "Unobtrusive Measures in Organizational Theory." *Administrative Science Quarterly, 24,* 650-659.

Weber, M. (1947). *The Theory of Social and Economic Organization.* A. Henderson and T. Parsons (Eds.). Glencoe: Free Press.

Weingast, B. (1984). "The Congressional Bureaucratic System: A Principal-Agent Perspective." *Public Choice, 44,* 147-191.

Weingast, B., & Moran, M. (1983). "Bureaucratic Discretion or Congressional Control." *Journal of Political Economy, 91,* 765-780.

Weiser, B. & McAllister, B. (1997, February 12). "The Little Agency That Can't." *Washington Post,* pp. A01.

West, W. (1995). "Controlling The Bureaucracy." *Theory and Practice.* Armonk: M.E. Sharpe.

White, J., & Adams, G. (Eds.). (1994). *Research in Public Administration.* Thousand Oaks: Sage.

Wildavsky, A. (1972). "The Self-Evaluating Organization." *Public Administration Review, 32,* 509-520.

Wildavsky, A. (1988). *The New Politics of the Budgetary Process.* Boston: Little, Brown.

Williamson, O. (1990). *Organization Theory.* New York: Oxford University Press.

Williamson, O. (1996). *The Mechanisms of Governance.* New York: Oxford University Press.

Williamson, O., & Winter, S. (Eds.). (1993). *The Nature of the Firm: Origins, Evolution, and Development.* New York: Oxford University Press.

Wilson, J. (Ed.). (1980). *The Politics of Regulation.* New York: Basic Books.

Wilson, J. (1989). *Bureaucracy.* New York: Basic Books.

Wilson, W. (1887). "The Study of Administration." *Political Science Quarterly, 2,* 197-222.

Wood, B., & Waterman, R. (1994). *Bureaucratic Dynamics.* Boulder: Westview Press.

Worsham, J., Eisner, M., & Ringquist. (1997). "Assessing the Assumptions: A Critical Analysis of Agency Theory." *Administration & Society, 28,* 419-440.

Wright, J. (1985). PACs, Contributions, and Roll Calls. American Political Science Review, 79, 400-414.

Zaller, J. (1992). *The Nature and Origins of Mass Opinion.* New York: Cambridge University Press.

Zogby International. *America Poll.* December 10-13, 1998.

Author Index

Subject Index